CUSTOMER SERVICE & INNOVATION IN LIBARIES

GLENN MILLER

THE HIGHSMITH PRESS HANDBOOK SERIES

Highsmith
PRESS
Fort Atkinson, Wisconsin

he Orange County Library System

Published by Highsmith Press LLC
W5527 Highway 106
P.O. Box 800
Fort Atkinson, Wisconsin 53538-0800

1-800-558-2110

© Glenn Miller, 1996

Cover art: Mary Ann Highsmith

The paper used in this publication meets the minimum requirements of
American National Standard for Information Science —
Permanence of Paper for Printed Library Material.
ANSI/NISO Z39.48-1992.

Library of Congress Cataloging-in Publication Data

Miller, Glenn
    Customer service & innovation in libraries / Glenn Miller.
        p.   cm. -- (The Highsmith Press handbook series)
    Includes index.
    ISBN 0-917846-39-7 (pbk : alk. paper)
    1. Libraries and readers--United States. I. Title. II. Series.
Z711.M54 1996
025.5'2774--dc20   95-53261

CONTENTS

FOREWORD

Everywhere two or more librarians are gathered these days, the conversation is bound to turn to the uncertain future of libraries. Proffered solutions tend to center around technology. Though it may certainly be a cornerstone for the future, technology should be emphasized as a means and not an end. Libraries should continue to emphasize basic services such as answering questions and circulating materials. These services can be enhanced and improved by technology, but they cannot be replaced by it. Accessing an online library catalog and learning that a book is owned or on the shelf is not the same as getting that book into the patron's hands. Service delivery must be taken one step further. Providing digitized books online might be one alternative in the future, but why not start today by getting material into the patron's hands in their home?

This work asks these questions and proposes methods for taking library service beyond the commonplace: Not just shelving books, but shelving them in a way that works for patrons and staff and not against them. Circulating books to patrons, but at their convenience–not at the library's. Helping patrons before they are forced to come to a desk to seek help. These are simple concepts but they're not widely practiced in today's libraries.

This book is also about throwing out traditional concepts and actively challenging the status quo. Acknowledging that today's library needs to adapt to changing conditions is the first step, but it is not enough. Experimentation, exploration, and acceptance that we are not limited by what has always been done before is key.

DEBBIE MOSS
ASSISTANT DIRECTOR
ORANGE COUNTY LIBRARY SYSTEM

PREFACE

It has often seemed that most of the literature on library administration that attracted my interest was written by theorists, teachers, or academic library managers. Public library directors did not often contribute to the professional literature, at least commensurate to their influence. Little was available that seemed to be wholly appropriate to my job. It may well have been due to myopia. It might also be something in the makeup of the library manager. Management meant that something was being conducted and that the product would be continuously improved.

Library administration is difficult work and the road is fraught with stumbling blocks. In a bureaucracy, change often troubles people, seemingly at every level. A stable work environment with a minimum of change appears to placate people, and it will draw less criticism or opposition. This book is about change and innovation. It was written in large measure because if the practitioners were doing it, they weren't writing about it. There were things being tried and

implemented at the Orange County Library System that didn't seem common among other libraries. A vibrant management environment had been created. There were successes and failures. It appeared that if this book was not written, some of these ideas would be permanently lost.

The community, the users, the staff, the managers, the Board and the government at all levels are the people of substance who contributed to this book. Don Sager, Highsmith Press, was the catalyst who said "why not" at the opportune time. A tolerant family permitted it to happen through the months. Every aspect of the author's library experience bears some responsibility for this book, and thus some of the blame.

1   CHANGE, INNOVATION & CUSTOMER SERVICE

As this country grew, we built our towns and cities so that they were convenient for walking. When public libraries came into existence, we walked to them. Public libraries became a source of education to be cherished as symbols of cultural goodness and as a result, we built more of them. As caretakers of these institutions, librarians bought and preserved more books so that the community wouldn't find itself apart from these valuable resources that brought self-improvement, education, and culture.

Times have changed. We don't walk to many places anymore, and there's too much communication for many people to be profoundly influenced by symbols. Resources for self-improvement are everywhere. While the public library was created by the people for the people, the public will let it go when and if they don't have use or want it anymore. Libraries have no absolute charter. If the public library is to continue to exist, then the library will necessarily have to develop and serve its customers in the ways they desire. It will not happen the other way around. The public is not going to conform to the direction or will of the public library. The public library is of the public, neither apart from it nor superior to it.

This is not an easy concept for many librarians. We may not feel as though our personal behavior has any particular influence on the public. We are just an infinitesimal part of the body politic, a small fish in a big pond. On the other hand, librarians are an important component of any change that happens at the public library, a relatively big fish in a small pond. There may be some conceptual sameness in the roles but there is no comparison in the relative impact. If we do nothing different in society, society changes anyway. If we do nothing different in our libraries, society does not remain unchanged, for it changes anyway. Unfortunately, I believe we have done very little that is different in our libraries in recent decades, and we are losing touch with our present and prospective customers. Libraries are going to have to change to adapt to the society. Society is not going to change to adapt to our libraries.

Libraries are affected by suburbanization, parking, multimedia formats, computers, escalators, among many other factors. For example, we seldom walk to our destinations. Our perceptions of institutions based on their symbolic former roles are no longer valid. Books are produced as readily as any other commodity, and self-improvement opportunities are at every hand. There can be little doubt why public library funding is under attack. In many states, cities and funding agencies, and library schools arc cither changing or going out of business. Without dramatic change, the public library is in for an unpleasant and uncertain future.

This book is about change in the public library. Many public libraries are threatened with financial insecurity. Yet many have existed for decades without any particular motivation to change. The result is that many inefficient processes have developed, and those responsible for them need to carefully re-examine their purposes. The selected examples in the chapters that follow represent dramatic departures from that which we have come to accept as the method or the objective of public library service. Consider them not as alternatives or adjustments to the accepted method as much as an entirely different way of thinking about achieving our goals.

Further, this book is about the role of individuals in the library organization at many levels. Change comes from individuals. While managers may have a broader role, all employees have insights and differing views of the organization. Accept that change is necessary. Become an agent who fosters change. Become someone who is able to get out in front of the crowd and

become an innovator. The innovators are the individuals who will not only capitalize on change but will revive the institution with increased efficiency.

One requirement of innovation is the ability or knack of recognizing opportunity. If we are going to change, then we must have a sense of what, where and how we should change. We also need to review why change is needed. Develop methods of feedback and dialogue with all the library's customers and staff. Examine customer use patterns and preferences. Examine how service is provided, and then consider and test an array of alternatives.

Every organization ought to have some form of a suggestion box, some way any person, staff or customer, can routinely comment on likes and dislikes. These messages are the stuff that dreaming and innovation are all about. Verbal comments, even complaints, can offer something different, something which you hadn't considered before, if you let it. You are not the only person who knows how to think. However, you may be in the unique position to assimilate concerns, mission and resources to come up with combinations and possibilities that raise the potential of doing more or doing something different and better.

Change is more than adding efficiency to what is already being done. Although that is a high ranking objective, it is not necessarily a separate process. Creativity and innovation are not linear tasks. That is, don't expect to have a meeting at 9:00 a.m., clear your desk at 10:00 a.m., and then innovate at 11:00 a.m. The process of innovation lends itself to the messy prospect of being ready for change at all times.

2 GREETER

Public libraries should have a "greeter" at their front door. It is almost incomprehensible to think that an average citizen could find his or her way around an institution as complex as a reasonably-sized, modern public library without some knowledgeable help. Yet, there will seldom be someone on duty to provide this assistance in a public library.

Libraries have a comparatively short history when one considers the sweep of time or the centuries-long background of some of our civilization's older institutions. Conversely, if your family has been using public libraries for generations, then public libraries do have a remarkable sameness. The same basic rules and understanding will get you around most public libraries. Librarians pride themselves on their awareness of the principles of good building layout and the value of easy-to-use buildings. Basically, the people who are most familiar with the institution, the ones who use it the most, tend to take it for granted. Those two groups, regulars and employees, are the ones who may

be most easily lulled into assumptions and presumptions about what is there, where it should be, and how it works. To the extent that they have had better than average library experience somewhere, they may expect that all libraries will have logical and reasonable services.

It's the same with physical plant. By the time someone has walked past the elevator 100 times and has heard someone explain 50 times that the building plan was designed so that the public can see the elevator from the front door, someone may tend to take for granted that, not only is it there, but that anyone can see it from the front door.

WHAT DIRECTIONAL QUESTIONS TELL US

Does your library maintain records of directional questions? Ask yourself how much time is spent considering those questions and their implications for the overall operations? Directional questions are, for the most part, the simple result of having people in the building. If someone is in front of you and asks a question about a physical location, it arises as a result of their not knowing their way around the library. Who answers their questions? Normally it is some relatively high-paid staff member. This is hypothetically a waste of money. However, it is not the worst problem that is represented. The largest problem, and it gets progressively worse as the building increases in size and complexity, is that there are taxpayers who are wandering about looking for something and do not know where or how to find it.

APPROACHABILITY

This problem also relates to the ever-present concern of the reference librarian regarding approachability. Does the public feel comfortable approaching the staff? Many users often doubt that their questions are worthy of the librarian's time. How many people walk right past them because they don't wish to show how ignorant they are? How many librarians, consciously or unconsciously, are less than welcoming in their posture or demeanor? How many libraries, regardless of intent, have their resources organized in a fashion that is instinctively apparent to all who come in the door? Further, how many of the users are knowledgeable about available resources? Who knows what is available in our libraries? It is arguable that many public service staff are not sufficiently aware of their library's resources. How could we possibly expect that any appreciable number of users know how the library is organized?

That's why there are librarians. They assist, interpret and find things. As time goes on, the flavor and physical appearance of any

institution and its resources change. Librarians are on the inside, and they have the best prospects of staying fairly current on changes in their library. The users must learn from them.

INDIVIDUAL CUSTOMER SERVICE

Let's look at what may well be one of the most significant and endearing aspects of the public library as an institution. The public library still, in the face of all that society presents to it, deals with one person at a time. Libraries are able to pursue the notion that each person is different. We accept and deal with each person as an individual. Nonetheless, when we are charging through a day, we are frequently blissfully unaware that individuals have come and gone through our institution without being so much as seen or acknowledged. True, some prefer it that way, and we won't question the range of possible motives. It is worthwhile to point out that while many of the faithful (heavy users) prefer to find what they want by themselves, their favored resources and techniques may be from another period or another type of library.

UNLOCKING THE LIBRARY'S SERVICES

Given the dramatic changes in library resources, cooperative resource sharing procedures, the increasing use of computers in libraries, and the many different information formats that will be found in libraries, it is increasingly important that the user engage a knowledgeable librarian if the user is ever going to have full access to the breadth of the library's collections and services. For that reason it is desirable that every library possessing complex ser-

Illustration 2.1: The library's greeter on duty in the lobby.

vices and collections maintain a greeter at the entry.

All such libraries ought to have a staff member present in the lobby greeting every person who comes in the door. The greeter has a variety of important functions, and it is a very difficult role to execute. The greeter is not merely someone who stands in the entry and says hello. This is a position that can have a large impact on how the entire entry area works.

INITIAL IMPRESSIONS

A popular phrase which has been used in advertising commercials is, "You don't get a second chance to make a first impression." This truism is brutally obvious if you have experienced the frustrated user who is having a bad day, and the library is making it worse with confusion, snafus and defensiveness. Much of the time the outcome of a

potentially tense situation rests with our own disposition. If you come into a situation with an open mind, one that is willing to meet the concern half way, the chances are very good that you will avoid being frustrated. Let's meet them at the door with a smile and let them know that this institution is pleased they are here, and that our intent is a positive reception.

Let's communicate at the very first opportunity that we are pleasant, and that we know who we are serving. Indeed, if we work for them, then let's let them know that we realize it. The job is not just limited to offering a happy face. Some staff could welcome people for weeks without ever thinking past a friendly welcome. Others could welcome people and do more harm than good. Nonetheless, what the greeter looks like is significant. There must be no doubt about whether this person works for the library.

There should be no message T-shirt or casual play clothes on an effective greeter.

THE CRITICAL MOMENT

This staff member must be fully aware of the library's services, collections, policies, and facilities. A user may respond with a very specific question if he or she is greeted with "how can I help you today?" That is not the time to refer them to someone behind a counter. That is a critical moment, because the greeter is in a position to save the user's time and avoid frustration. If you ever had to meet a connecting flight in a busy and unfamiliar airport when your plane is late in arriving, then you may know just how wonderful it is to see the airline staff waiting to direct you to the desired gate for departure. It would be unreasonable to expect that the passengers are familiar with the schedule or the airport. In our case, just because we are familiar with the routines doesn't mean that very many library users are. Library buildings may be imposing but it is the staff that can make them functional for the user.

OTHER ROLES FOR THE GREETER

The functionality needn't stop there. Assuming the greeter is located near the front door, there are some other library services right at hand. Probably the circulation and book return functions are near. Since the greeter is knowledgeable about library services, let's also make that staff member knowledgeable about library policies and procedures, particularly those concerning the activities at the nearby counters. Then, if a circulation clerk needs clarification or some supervisory judgement is needed, the greeter is there to handle it. The supermarket check-out line provides some insight. If a clerk needs a supervisor to approve a check, the designated person is in the area. If they're not, the store's management ought to think about who's in line and who's paying the bills. In our case it's a taxpayer, of course.

The next need is participation in the ebb and flow of staffing the various desks and activities. If there is someone in the lobby who has the capacity to sense the volume of usage in different areas of the library, then that person is uniquely placed and qualified to judge the overall activity.

When a large number of users are ready to check out, additional lanes may be needed at the circulation desk. When there is a mechanical problem, the greeter may be able to take immediate action. If one station is quiet and another is swamped, a person on the scene can give prompt attention. When emergency arises, the greeter can step in and check out some material or register a borrower. This generalist can spot the burned-out bulb or the wet floor and immediately solve a potential problem or call for help. Who sets out the wet floor pylon in your lobby? And when?

Lobby host or hostess? Name the role what you will but this job is not being done very well right now in our libraries. The scope may sound broad but there are many staff members who can handle it. Not to leave out the obvious, the people in this role could wear a tailored blazer or something that would be obvious and yet tasteful. They can even pick out the color themselves (as long as all are the same). The users will want to know who they can look to for help and something distinctive will surely help. Not only will it help, but the staff wearing the blazer will know that they have a spotlight on them, and the authority to go with it.

SECURITY

There is also a subtle social role that a greeter naturally assumes. We have no idea about what's on the mind of the individuals coming into the library. Most are availing themselves of the institution's services. Some of them are passing time. Each person who comes in knows why they're there and whether or not they wish to be anonymous. If an individual does not wish to be noticed, that individual probably will avoid a building where someone is clearly in a position to see each and every person who enters. This doesn't portend anything dramatic or evil, but it does suggest that some individuals might find the library less attractive.

I know that I would like to have a greeter in a large and complex public service building. I am convinced that the role fills a useful public purpose. Doubtless, this is an innovation which is already accommodated in some libraries. Greet the people who are paying our salaries. Let them know that we want to help them. Save them some steps or from uncertainty. Improve the ambience of the entry/lobby. Be proactive in your relationship with the library's users.

3 SHELVING MAINTENANCE

Books on library shelves should be easy to use and attractive to the eye. Unfortunately, that is not the case in some libraries. Shelf maintenance is a remarkable example of library complacency. Libraries have permitted their resources, their stock in trade, to fall into a condition that can be described as either difficult to use or an unattractive conglomeration of books. Libraries must take greater care in shelving, and one way to do it is to see the book shelves through the eyes of the users. Books are not shelved in a way that is convenient for library users. We can easily change this and improve the accessibility to the library's collections while we reduce the cost of maintenance.

Many librarians tend to take books for granted. Books that have made it back to the shelves get little attention. But if we want to better serve the users, we need to take a fresh look at the way bookshelves are used. Most people who remove books from library shelves do so without telling library staff how they could arrange them better. It probably doesn't even occur to them. They use the books as they find them and generally do not share their observations with anyone. If they had a problem, the library probably didn't hear about it.

Illustration 3.1: How accessible are the books on the top shelf for this user?

USER ACCESS

Watch the users when they do take books off the shelves. Most people who use libraries are of average height and possess average physical capabilities. There is a distinct relationship to their height and their ease of accessibility to the books. If users have bifocals, it is just not easy to see the book details on the upper or lower shelves. If they have any physical limitation at all, it may be nearly impossible to get to the bottom or the top shelves.

THE NEW MOON SYNDROME

Because of these variables, depending on the initiative and instructions to the shelvers, there is a condition that can be called the "new moon" syndrome. When you look at sections of shelving, and you see that there are shelves in the middle of the section which have fewer books than those shelves at the top or bottom, you are being acquainted with the "new moon" syndrome. Over time, normal library users and users with differing physical attributes will tend to take books from the shelves they can best see and reach. If we have books that are out of reach, we have books that are less likely to be examined or checked out.

To the extent that it is easier to reach empty space on shelves than it is to reach books, we are doing the shelving for some reason other than the convenience of the library's users. The rationalizations and explanations given for this phenomenon are plentiful. There are too many books. There isn't enough shelving. There aren't enough shelvers. Weeding takes too much time. The public wants more books on the shelves, not fewer. It doesn't matter. Nobody cares.

Have you ever worked for an hour at a counter or sink that is too short for you? Bending at your hips, however slightly, is an unnatural position for your back. Does a librarian bend over ten or one hundred times each day examining books on the shelves? Two hundred days in a year and ten years suggests that a librarian may bend over 200,000 times during this period. You might think this is no problem, if you're healthy. How about the shelver, who by the same deduction may bend over 500 or a 1,000 times a day? That's bending over 50,000 times in a year? We might consider this when lamenting the turnover, health, and burnout of shelvers.

It is a truism that we notice things that are wrong more than we notice things that are right. Usually, we just take things for granted. This is certainly applicable in the library. If you should notice four or five people in the book stacks and note that none are bending over, ask yourself if it is a coincidence or is your material actually on the shelves where it is convenient to the user. Or, are the ones who are on the floor young and fit, or do they tend to be middle age and above? Does anyone comment? Seldom. If one could eliminate most of the bending in library bookstacks, over time, individuals might have fewer visits to the doctor.

Shelvers would almost certainly work more efficiently, which would lead to significant savings for everyone. It is unlikely that any of the groups would be conscious of the difference. We have a very strong tendency to take things for granted. Change is not easy, though, and we will find reasons to continue doing things the same way that we have done them in the past. One of the barriers to change is the belief that empty library shelves must be avoided. Every time we depend upon comparative statistics which say that more books are better than fewer books, we shoot ourselves in the foot.

THE IMPORTANCE OF WEEDING

We need to realize that public libraries are not in the collecting business anymore; they are in the *using* business. If the books are not being used, get them out of the way. All the users would find it easier to locate their material. Every shelver will be a better worker. Librarians would be more efficient in working with the collection. If most users examine books on the shelves, and most of the staff work with books on the shelves regularly, then the amount of wasted time and energy must be prodigious if all must handle or consider books which few people, if any, ever borrow.

Librarians are good at rationalizing. They take great pains to suggest to the world that if someone takes a book off the shelf they have provided a service. This is wrong if we have merely required the user to wade or plow through many irrelevant books looking for one that hits the mark. Of course, there are no absolutes and it is arguable that the books each have their particular user. Certainly history books require different attention than fiction. Regardless, if that argument justifies keeping all the old, unused books on our shelves, we need a wake-up call. Collecting for a future and hypothetical user will not be supported by public library funding authorities. The benefits are hypothetical and minimal in the face of dramatically increasing costs. If a book isn't being used, get it out of the way.

Ruthless weeding based upon lack of use is a far more efficient use of time than thoughtful consideration book-by-book by high-priced staff. I'm not suggesting that there are no differences between various types of books or that judgement and common sense should be ignored. But the concept of fewer books on the shelves is consistent with shelving that is better for the user and taxpayer.

SHELVING TO INCREASE ACCESS

What do the books look like if they are all in the middle of the shelving section? They may look like they are there on purpose. From a distance they look orderly and accessible. If they're not right, anybody can see it instinctively. Assume that a section of book shelving is about 70" high. A normal section would hold six shelves plus the base, which also could hold books. Arbitrarily, number them from the top, one through seven. The two most easily accessible shelves (numbers two and three) should be filled loosely from end to end without a bookend. The shelves above and below those should be empty. If there are more books than can fit loosely, the next lower shelf (number four) should be partially filled and have a bookend to hold the books up since these are the ones which absorb the ebb and flow of borrowing. Do not put bookends on the primary shelves. Bookends would just be in the way and provide justification for shelvers to leave unused space on those shelves. The primary shelves should have books somewhat loose so that additional volumes can be easily added, and to avoid difficulty in removing books. If books have to be moved to an adjacent or lower shelf, so be it, for that's

Illustration 3.2: Improving user access to materials requires leaving the upper and lower shelves empty.

what shelf maintenance is all about. We do this for the user, not for ourselves.

If there is some uncertainty about the relative height of the shelves, adjust them. It's a simple act to adjust most library shelves. Keep in mind that from a distance a range of shelving looks better if the shelves are all lined up horizontally. Aesthetics may not be paramount, but it certainly affects the way users and staff react in the long run.

Even relatively short people will find that their eyes are closer to the traditional spine label on shelf number two than on shelf number four. Further, for most people, it is more convenient to raise their arm a few inches than to bend over. This does not mean that short people will need a kick-step stool to reach the uppermost books. The top shelf, (number one) shouldn't be used for shelving the collection. It is too high.

VARIATIONS IN SHELVING

Some judgement is needed if the relative height of the existing shelves defies the concept being described. Different parts of the

collection will require adjustments to this general description, such as the children's collection or large art books, compared with fiction or biography.

If a short person can see and reach up to shelf number two then it is also arguable that the taller person should not have to bend over to see books on shelves number five or six. The perception is that short people do not have to bend over to read and get the books on lower shelves, even shelf numbers four and five. This is wrong, for even short persons will have to bend over to see and read the spine label of books on shelf numbers four and five. We collect taxes from people without regard to their height, and therefore we ought to shelve the books so that everybody can use the books.

We are not accustomed to thinking this new way. Conventionally, if we have books, then shelve them. If we have space on shelves, use it. If the books look neat, then that's the way they should be. If the books are loose, then tighten them. Most public library

Illustration 3.3: Shelving adjusted too low for comfortable access.

Illustration 3.4: Shelving convenient for use.

book shelves look as though they receive regular attention. Some of them, on the other hand, look as though they hadn't been touched by staff in some time beyond adding books as they are returned. First impressions may be misleading. Sometimes a busy library will have stacks that look unkempt, and the quiet library has attractive and orderly books.

SHELVING MULTIPLE COPIES

Multiple copies are a concern for libraries that buy in quantity because there just isn't room for the extra copies on the shelves. This doesn't need to be a problem. In the previous configuration, the lower shelves are normally empty. Leave several copies of the popular title in their normal sequence, and put the extra copies apart from the normal sequence on a lower shelf, visually

and physically separated from the other copies. It is immediately obvious to the user why the books are out of order, and it is not an inconvenience. Visually, the stacks still look good and functionally, the staff has continuous and simple awareness of titles that could bear some supplemental attention.

SHELVER TRAINING

Some may say that full shelves make for inconvenient shelving and loose books are much more likely to be pushed through. This is not necessarily true. When training the shelvers, do not teach anyone to shelve books with one hand while the other hand carries more books to shelve. One-handed shelving results in a tendency to push books through to the other side. Happily, when some empty shelves are waist high, it pro-

Illustration 3.5: Train shelvers to avoid shelving with one hand in order to avoid pushing books through to the other side of the shelf sections.

vides an easy place to set the extra books down while using two hands to shelve the current book. Keeping books loose on the full shelves means that a book or two can be shelved there without having to move books to other shelves. Sometimes there is a tendency to cram books tight whether or not a book end is employed.

If it helps to visualize the overall process and result, think of shelf maintenance as a way to move empty shelf space out of the way of the user in favor of making books more convenient to see, reach and shelve. A great deal of what librarians do is related to adding, removing, and replacing books on the shelves. The way libraries do it has survived because it is seldom challenged. The next time you are in your supermarket, notice the order and maintenance. They have competition, libraries do not.

EFFECTIVE USE OF STAFF

Libraries must change the way they maintain bookstacks in favor of methods which are more efficient. Since it is unlikely that others will consider this to be a problem, librarians must take the initiative. The library's funding authority isn't likely to delve into the detail of our operations, but they are developing records on personnel efficiency.

There are few repetitive operations that are as pervasive in the conduct of library service than removing and returning books to shelves. Minute improvements can have dramatic savings both for the user in convenience and for the taxpayer in cost. Libraries must re-examine the methods employed in shelving and stack maintenance.

4 STORYTELLING

Storytelling has a long and treasured history. It is a centerpiece of communication down through the ages. Public libraries have a good record of using and preserving the art of storytelling compared to other institutions. Unfortunately, storytelling is not being used to its full potential in public library service, and changes are required to meet current and future needs.

Public libraries have given so many storytimes over the years that it would take a long time for any other institution to exceed that acknowledged leadership, particularly among those of us who are devoted to reading. Public libraries have been the site of millions of storytime presentations. Of everything public libraries do, nothing is as natural, charming, and loved as the children's story hour, and the pride of parents and caregivers as they observe their children develop an appreciation of good literature. It has been a natural arena for libraries. Few services we offer are as popular as the storytime. Libraries are, after all, advocates for the children. No other institu-

tion, other than the schools, is as closely associated with the early development of children as the public library. Actually, there are other caregivers that have made great strides, such as the Head Start program, but they have such complex challenges.

What are we really doing? In most cases, we have taken traditional storytelling and turned it into an adequate presentation with any number of techniques and devices that serve our purposes. To be sure, there are countless children's librarians who are simply marvelous and very skilled at basic and fundamental storytelling. They share themselves in a selfless way and are to be congratulated on delightful performances. Most storytimes last 15-30 minutes and provide a learning experience predicated on engaging the children, introducing a story, doing a finger play, manipulating a hand puppet, and chanting a nursery rhyme.

Based on my discussions with children's librarians, it takes four or five hours of librarian time to prepare for a storytime of twenty minutes duration, and it takes eight to ten hours to memorize one story for delivery to the children. These observations are not pejorative in nature. They are merely reasonable estimates of what is taking place.

Regardless of our motivations, most libraries have limited resources. We would prefer to offer constant story experiences for any children who might show up. We have always felt that way. We would like to have a personal repertoire of dozens of memorized stories which we would perform at the drop of a hat. We would like to be free to concentrate on only that in the course of a day. We would like it if the children would come in droves to take advantage of our services. We would like these things, but we must be realistic about just what we could accomplish in a day. We have to be realistic about promise and fulfillment. Storytimes don't just happen.

The children who come to library story hours are relatively few. That is, relative to the potential numbers, we see just a small proportion of the children, especially on any repeat basis. Large numbers of children, when present, are usually there when someone brings them on a bus. If they arrive by bus, the experience is filled with so many extraneous and logistical details that much is lost in the process. The learning experience is provided. What cannot be offered are the inspirational and repeated contacts which provide a lasting desire on the part of the children to get more. This desire is ultimately what motivates children to read, to open their minds, to learn how to learn, to give their minds a glimpse of their potential.

We aren't having that impact on children anymore; at least not to the extent we once did. The believers in the children's literature experience are managing to get their children to the storytimes, wherever they are. The children who are bused are there a few times because the schedules got arranged, but it's unlikely they will be back on a regular basis. Maybe it's just the remarkable changes in society. More people want their children to participate but it is just not feasible logistically. Demands are just too great and everybody is just too busy. There is also the local library's funding challenges, which may affect the frequency of their children's programming.

On the other hand, maybe the public library ought to change in concert with the needs of its users. Who has not noticed that Barney, Reading Rainbow, Sesame Street, Mr. Rogers and other children's programs are available generously throughout the day? Is there a children's librarian who isn't acquainted with the content of these programs? Has the availability of these programs reduced the need for library children's programming? Wringing our hands is one obvious reaction. What can we do about this apparent lessening of respect and need for the library?

Start with the notion that libraries are here for the children and their parents instead of the opposite. We can make it easier to use and take advantage of public library services. In the case of storytimes, the most common denominator is that if children are brought to the library we will expose them to good literature and media.

Notwithstanding that many story experiences are taken to remote sites, the public still must bring their children to us. How else can we envision this relationship? Well, if we wish to be more convenient then why must the public come to us? If the user has multiple things to do and not enough time to do them, guess what suffers? When you are running errands and there isn't enough time, what do you do? You don't make it to all of them, you don't do all the errands. Some combination of urgency, need and convenience enters the process and without dwelling on it, we make an unconscious decision. Increasingly we don't make the library trip. Why not? It takes time; it requires the children; it is located in a problematic place; parking may be a problem; who knows when there will be a story hour?

It gets easier and easier to understand why people don't make it to the library, regardless of their desires and intentions. How do librarians respond to this? One response is to find ways of providing storytelling with methods, times and places which are easy and convenient to the public. We need to do that without sacrificing efficiency. We need to do it in a less expensive manner. We need to do it without sacrificing quality. The experience needs to be more attractive from a cost/benefit perspective. If we wait, there are elected officials who will make the decision for us.

Let's look at the significant components of storytelling independently and then consider them together.

STAFF

Generally speaking, the staff who actually conduct storytimes are library service providers in the broad sense and programmers in a more narrow role. If storytelling for our children is worth the effort, then it war-rants being conducted by staff who have no other burdens or concerns.

Our storytelling should be conducted by competent performers whose full time is devoted to creating and delivering their stories. When stories are developed and learned, the maximum number of children should benefit.

Consider the notion of storyteller as opposed to storytime librarians. Most storytimes in this country are given by motivated persons who have little or no specialized training or experience in storytelling. We hire individuals to provide a public library program; some of them have a penchant for storytelling. Should a child be entertained by one of us reading a story, manipulating a puppet, dramatizing a character, or would it be better to be enchanted by a storyteller? Note that I have not said that the children do not benefit from the experiences which librarians have given them. There are many learning experiences the staff can offer that will be invaluable to the child in future years. By focusing on these areas, whether it pertains to learning how to find resources in the library or gaining skills in evaluating books, children's librarians can enrich the young people they serve.

AUDIENCE

All the children of the community are the potential audience for our storytelling. These are the same children who are not regularly driven to the library by their parents and cannot walk to our libraries. If they come, they will show up at someone else's prerogative. They will be brought to us by someone who has less and less time and opportunity to do so. Depending on scheduling, they may also be brought by school bus or day care van.

Why would anyone be surprised if the attendance by children at public library storytimes is problematical and declining at some of our buildings? Where are these children and how might we have access to them in ways that are easier for parents and caregivers? If we consider these questions we may be able to increase attendance. Where can the stories be told that would be easier for the drivers? Where are the parents when they are in their cars with the children? They're probably at the grocery, doctor, school, mall, cleaners, druggist, post office, and numerous other destinations which have a lot to do with the roads and not much to do with library locations.

Further, there isn't much time between those various activities. Every minute counts. How many minutes does it take to go to the library and check out some books? It requires a lot of time to dress the children, pack them in the car, drive to the library, circle the block, find a parking space, shepherd the children, navigate to the front door, guide the children to the book treasures, umpire their choices of books, and then repeat the routine to reach home. It is no longer an easy, nurturing trip. Because of the complexity of today's society, a trip to the library must be planned among competing forces. It is arguable that even now the library loses the competition more than it wins. The children can't get to us by themselves.

LOCATION

There is nothing startling about the fact that most public library storytimes take place inside the library building. Some-times we have lovely rooms designed and built for that purpose. Other times you can watch the storytime as it occurs in open library spaces because we don't have the luxury of special rooms. Some storytimes are travelling to more remote places in the community. For example, some programs are given in day care centers and other places where children are found. If the objective is to offer literature-based learning experiences for children, and we expect literature to become an integral part of their lives, then maybe we ought to be putting the programs into a more normal environment for the drivers and caregivers. Maybe we ought to be bringing story programs to children where we can find them in groups of any description. After all, we are mobile and the children are not. Rather, we can be mobile if we choose to be, the children cannot.

ELIMINATING THE BARRIERS TO CHILDREN'S SERVICES

We must to have the courage to look at the barriers that prevent children from benefiting from storytelling and all our other services, and find a way around or over those barriers. One alternative is to develop a cadre of storytellers from among those who now conduct storytimes. Select those who are the best at it and who have the stamina and motivation to nothing else in the course of a day. The salaries would comes from the existing personnel budget. Provide a manager who can successfully balance people, schedules and locations in a meaningful and efficient way. Provide all storytelling from a centrally scheduled group of dedicated storytellers. Lease space in a good traffic location that has ample parking. Remodel the space into a number of acoustically appropriate story/meeting rooms with primary consideration for the easy ingress and egress of groups of children. Plan carefully for near-continuous storytelling, allowing one group to follow another or overlap while avoiding conflicts between groups entering and exiting.

Be creative, use velour ropes and stanchions to collect participants for the next storytelling program. At the same time, guide those exiting to a reasonable gathering or meeting spot. The family car or the school bus should be able to come and go with a minimum of difficulty. The distance from the parking lot should be minimal. The programs should start at frequent intervals during the prime hours of the day. At night or during slow times, the rooms can be used for regular meeting space within library rules.

OTHER RELATED SERVICES

Don't miss the opportunity to test other library services, especially if they might relate to children's services. Put a browsing library in the same building with children's books of the sort that are being utilized for the programs. Minimize the chairs but do include a speaker system to page the browsing parent whose child is out of the story room and ready to go. Put in an island like the movie theater's snack bar. From such a place you could check out books, supervise the area, sell paperback editions of the storytelling classics and be a clearing house for information on future programs or new services.

DRIVE-UP SERVICE

Did you add a drive-up window? Don't wait to copy this idea from a giant bookstore. Offer parents the opportunity to borrow pre-packaged children's and adult books without getting out of the car. Each package would include a selection of recent and classic titles of various types. It's not for all of us, but then everybody doesn't see the world just as we do.

Children are essential to our mission and there is no reason to lose them due to societal changes. However, there is a need to review what we are doing for children and to assess its effectiveness. Our users are conducting their lives differently from what they did 20 or 40 years ago. In contrast, public libraries are conducting children's services the same way they did 20 or 40 years ago. Whether you read budgets, statistics, cards or straws in the wind, public libraries need to change the way they deliver service to children. It's no longer working for a majority of this nation's children, and we would rather not hear about it. The children's service paradigm in the public library is ready for some shifting.

5 BOOKSTORE

Bookstores and libraries have much in common. Frequently their users are the same. Their functions are compatible and complementary, and for those reasons a public library of any size should have a used bookstore. Of course, another reason is that a used bookstore can generate money, but money is not its greatest value. A bookstore can provide both service to users and remarkable logistical support to the library. The services and support are worth more than the cash.

Now, that ought to be provocative. Libraries should sell used books from among the gifts they receive and also from the collection as library value has subsided or passed. They should sell them to the public, but the money is not the primary reason for doing so. That statement would seem to fly in the face of many very exciting library book sales around the country, most often conducted by a local Friends of the Library organization. The general impression is that money

raised is used for the direct support and benefit of the parent public library. Indeed, most book sales probably accomplish just that–a hard-earned windfall of cash which buys new books or equipment.

If and when a public library reaches a certain size, it takes on special characteristics. It changes into a business enterprise which rises and falls, in large measure, on the efficiency and effectiveness of the organization. In other words, the magnitude of its budget, staff, physical plant, array of services and complexity require that the parts of such an organization be thoroughly integrated into a single machine. If successful, all of the parts of this machine will be attuned to one another in a way that they are mostly interdependent; each is designed to blend with the rest so that not only the parts but the whole is efficient. It is pursuing its goals but it is doing so in a fashion that resists viewing any part separate from the others in effort or in plan.

THE ROLE OF THE LIBRARY BOOKSTORE

A bookstore is in a special position to assist significantly in various library roles. To the extent that a bookstore is seen as an operation that is distinct from the library, many efficiencies and opportunities are lost. This is specially true when management of the library and of the bookstore are distinct from one another. A volunteer organization seldom has patience or energy for absorbing the sometimes assiduous detail of management. To make more money than the year before is quite honorable enough and it is a goal that can be understood by all. Indeed, it is entirely positive.

Once a used bookstore reaches that critical mass of viability, myriad actions are required on a continual basis. The library needs to solicit used books, actively or passively. The books need to be transported to a central point. Some gifts are collections which have to be picked up by appointment. All gifts need to be reviewed by the library in some fashion. Valuable and/or usable books ought to be examined for library use, however cursory the examination. Sorting should be done too. Transportation happens again as sorted gifts go their various ways–to the trash, to acquisitions for the collection, to other nonprofit organizations, and to the bookstore as stock. The bookstore portion of the gifts are classified, priced, shelved and sold. Money is counted, protected, deposited and reported. The store is furbished and refurbished, changed and adjusted. Allied products like T-shirts and calendars are created, added, advertised, stored, and sold.

The bookstore is a natural extension of the simple, straightforward book sale. But what is required to integrate it with the library, and how do the pieces fit together? The library solicits books from the community. Some folks, but not all, automatically think of the public library when they have a need to get rid of their books. Thus, books will show up at library agencies regardless of how aggressively the library solicits gifts. Often gifts can be viewed as a either a benefit or as a problem. If they come one or two books at a time, they probably will come across the circulation desk. These represent no problem, and they are set aside and moved to a central place as time permits.

HANDLING LARGER DONATIONS

The larger quantity of gift books will arrive in greater numbers. Because of the quantity, there must be some convenient and accessible place for the donor to leave them. Short of significant signage, there must be a logical drop-off location which is part of the library and which permits the donor to feel that the staff has visual control of the spot. It is fairly important that the donor can drop off books/boxes and leave without having to speak to anyone. It is important that staff not be interrupted from other public service activities if the donor doesn't need the contact. So, when picking a drop-off location pick one on the loading dock or by the back door where the donor can drive up, preferably with overhead protection. You want them to leave the packages and drive away without undue handling of the books or the feeling that staff must deal with them right that second lest the books be missed or stolen.

Unfortunately, the stage is set for frustration because some of the offerings will be so dirty or disreputable that nobody wants to touch them. These gifts probably shouldn't even be brought inside. Leave them outside until that much of a determination can be made. Hopefully, the dumpster or the recycling bin is in the same area, simplifying dumping some or all of a box or boxes right into it.

The converse is also true, for some donations will include very attractive new books of great value to the library's collections. For that reason the deposit location should be within visual control. Desirable gifts should not be left unattended. Employees, as well as passersby, are susceptible to temptation. Another good reason to have visual control of the area is to offer the donors some satisfaction the library knows the gift is there. Some may even wish to have a receipt.

DONOR RECEIPTS

The receipt is a reasonable request and should be met. The library is merely acknowledging receipt of an estimated number of books. The donor can take responsibility for assigning value. There will be occasions when the donor wants a receipt listing specific books, title by title. If at all possible, accommodate such a request. Rejection may result in bad public relations which have a tendency to compound. The manner in which the library accepts donations says a great deal about the institution's attitude toward the public.

The public will also have questions about what the library will accept, ranging from books to stacks of magazines, for example. If at all possible, accept them because it is helpful to the individual taxpayer. If they call about the library's willingness to receive material, encourage them to drop it off and

most will. If they cannot or will not, try to accommodate them. If at all possible, arrange to pick up their donation. Frequently someone is closing a house or moving. It might be easier for them to put the books in the trash. But if you want the public, especially those involved in closing an estate, to have a clearly positive image of the library as a depository for collections of used books, it is worth the time to be gracious. It is difficult to predict what material will sell in the bookstore. When talking with donors, be sure to ask the size of boxes the gifts will be in or determine whether the library must bring boxes to accommodate the gifts. People who are getting rid of books may fill a huge box that can't be picked up or they may fill the trunk of their car with loose books. Graciousness and a dose of self-effacement by the library will pay off.

STORAGE OF GIFTS

It is probably already apparent that branches and remote locations are going to be depositories for gift books, just like the main facility. All of them are involved already with delivery but in this case, priorities must be considered. The gift books can be stored for a time, depending on space, and picked up only when there are sufficient numbers or there is nothing of a higher priority waiting. This could mean that gift books could sit around for a while. Gift books are not at the top of the library mission; do not make the mistake of forgetting why we are going to work each day.

Direct costs for dealing with gift books should be avoided in favor of incidental efforts. Specific routines should be minimized in favor of piggybacking on procedures which are ongoing.

Assuming that the books are being periodically collected and brought to a central point, another issue arises. There may not be sufficient room to save gift books for occasional sorting. Like everything else, choices have to be made. For the sake of efficiency someone has to decide whether gifts will be sorted, how they will be sorted and by whom. It is very desirable that a regular routine be established. Do not let gift books pile up until they pose a daunting sight. At the point that gifts become a negative concern to the staff, the overall utility of the concept is damaged. Manage the flow of gifts so that handling them is a routine instead of a project. Sort them regularly, throwing away the junk and moving the rest to the next step.

EFFICIENT SORTING

Sorting gift books may be an appropriate job for rare book curators but it's one that most libraries must do with clerical staff. It is not worth the cost in public money to assign professional staff to handle all gifts just because of the possibility that an occasional gift may be valuable. In the first place, it is problematic that a professional, under these circumstances, will catch the possible rare book, if indeed such books are present. Would an owner knowingly discard a valuable book? Secondly, there will be so many books that the sort at this point must be cursory. It must be done quickly.

The library will need to develop a simple set of standards employees can use to sort the books. If volunteers are doing this, they must be made aware that time is of the essence. (Keith Crotz has written a concise

guide for volunteers on sorting and pricing gift books in *Used Book Sales: Less Work & Better Profits* [Highsmith Press, 1995].)

GIFT BOOK CATEGORIES

The standards set in each library will doubtless vary and change from time to time. One model standard starts with a choice of end intentions for the books: (1) books to discard forthwith; (2) a limited number of books in very good condition, including current books, for professional library evaluation; (3) books for bookstore processing which comprises the bulk of the gifts, and (4) books for separation into boxes for secondary donation to other non-profit organizations.

Some of the gifts are presented by donors who have no background with books and are driven mostly by a desire to get rid of them. Most librarians have seen such gifts. Dead or alive insects, droppings, yellowed paper, irrelevant junk, dirt and grease are pretty broad clues that the donations should go in the recycling bin or to the dumpster. If there is any doubt about throwing it away, resist the temptation to handle it and toss it with dispatch. Do not spend an extra penny of staff cost on it. Possibly someone may throw away something valuable but it's unlikely. Any other approach is too expensive.

One significant problem for every librarian is the withdrawn, discarded and defaced library book that appears in the gift box. Once owned by a library, it can reappear once again as a book rejected by the donor. Fortunately, this is not a frequent problem. One of the justifications for library book sales and used bookstores is the opportunity it grants the public to buy good books at a nominal cost. The process eliminates criticism that the library is arbitrarily discarding materials. The library can also recoup at least some of the cost. This underlines the fact that profit is not the primary motivation for a used bookstore. The library can methodically weed and withdraw books, resulting in a systematic way to get more books in the pipeline to the bookstore.

GIFTS OF GREATER VALUE

Donors occasionally contribute books which are in very good condition and unique in some special fashion. They may be familiar titles, or impressive "coffee table" books, or a collection of seldom used books on a common theme or subject. If there is something pleasantly unusual about some gifts, set them aside for further evaluation. Remember, if there is doubt about a choice, put them into the lower, less desirable of the categories and do it quickly.

By far the largest group to be isolated are the titles which are going to the bookstore. They are the books in reasonable condition, fiction and nonfiction, which will comprise the basic stock of the bookstore. They will be the majority of the books to be sorted, and the ones that didn't fit the other categories.

SECONDARY GIFTS

The fourth sorting category is one which becomes easier to identify over time. Experience will provide some guidance. These are the titles that would be too out-dated to be on a library shelf, and of limited salability in the bookstore. When a book has languished in the bookstore for a period of

time, say four to six months, it is time to get rid of it. That is not to say that the book has no value. Rather it says that if these books do not turn over, they are not worth keeping in this store. They should be donated to other nonprofit organizations that reach other groups of book buyers.

In most communities there are huge rummage sales and giant garage sales that are usually sponsored by nonprofit groups. They would appreciate ten or a hundred boxes of books to offer at nominal cost. Interior decorators sometimes purchase large quantities of books at these sales for aesthetic purposes. Restaurants and bars use books to provide an ambiance. If you are located in proximity to film or television production facilities there will be calls to see if they can beg, borrow or steal quantities of books for sets. There are nonprofit organizations that solicit books to supplement education in parts of the world or that seek temporary help following disasters. The library with a quantity of boxed books can often find a worthy recipient, and save some books from the landfill. If the library gives them away, they are called secondary gifts.

THE IMPORTANCE OF EFFICIENT OPERATING PROCEDURES

Every library will have a different set of standards for gift books. The categories are not that important. What is important is that this facet of the library's business be handled efficiently, and in a fashion that doesn't interfere with other library routines. Once the books make their way to the bookstore, they need to be prepared for sale. Ideally, volunteers should be recruited for this activity. If library staff must be used, the time devoted to classifying, pricing, labeling and shelving needs to be kept in balance, so this cost does not exceed potential revenue. The working space of the bookstore should be designed so that books move through it in a continuous and regular process. Books should be processed and shelved in the order they arrive. While they need to be arranged by subject or type of book for the ease of the potential buyers, effort should be made to group the books by the date they were added to the bookstore stock. Titles that do not sell should be regularly rotated out of the store, to allow space for other books to replace them. Books should not be stored in nooks and crannies, where they fall out of the normal display areas.

VOLUNTEERS

Ideally, the bookstore workers should be volunteers. They may be Friends of the Library, general volunteers, or members of community service clubs willing to donate time to the library for this project. Liaison with library management will also be essential to ensure that their work dovetails with other library procedures.

Bookstore organization clearly does not require that books be shelved by Dewey or Library of Congress classification. Subject groupings will change, depending in part who is doing it and the nature of the gifts. Obviously, subjects and types of books such as fiction and nonfiction need to be shelved together. However, the organization is not as crucial in a bookstore. The library may expend an amazing amount of energy in organizing its collection. The bookstore has no such need for detail or precision, as

long as the buyer can reasonably locate the general area of interest.

EFFECTIVE PRICING PROCEDURES

Pricing used books for sale is worthy of its own treatise. However, in a library bookstore, getting the maximum possible price for each book is not the objective. Moving more books at lower prices has much to recommend it. The more people who leave with more books at a time, the fewer books the library will have to deal with in some other way. If types of books can be priced generically, it will save time and effort.

For example, try a sign that states "all hardback books are $1 unless marked otherwise." The significant majority of hardback books are $1 and therefore do not even have to be marked. "All paperbacks are 3 for $1," is another option. That will eliminate the need to mark all the paperbacks, and this will save an enormous amount of time, and greatly increase the efficiency of the operation.

It may seem that this approach will not generate as much money, but greater profits can be realized by reducing operational costs. The experience in Orlando, Florida, may be enlightening. In less than ten years, with net proceeds increasing every year, using supervised volunteers for the performance of in-store tasks, the Friends have realized $120,000 in a year. Even if there were no profits, the store could be justified, because it would relieve paid staff of the responsibility and time required to withdraw and dispose of obsolete titles from the collection.

CASH HANDLING PROCEDURES

Handling cash is another complication in running a library bookstore. Any time money is involved in the library's operations there are factors that must be considered. Cash must be handled in a fashion which is accurate, credible, simple, easy and with stringent rules and standards. The library's fiscal responsibilities are great and a special magnifying glass is applied whenever state sales taxes are collected.

In operating a used bookstore, the money is going to be handled by many individuals who are mostly volunteers. Assuming the operation is successful, the amount of money will increase rapidly. Early planning is crucial to avoiding loss and confusion. The bookstore cannot be allowed to grow like topsy. Book sales revenues ought to be handled as nearly as possible as cash from fees and fines are handled by the library. The standards and oversight which the library enjoys are warranted in the bookstore. Have it grow with sound procedures.

BOOKSTORE APPEARANCE

Having done all the preparation and work to get the books as far as the bookstore, don't forget the store's design and appearance. The bookstore is as much a public service as the rest of the library. Whether it is in the main library or in the branches, it should look like the library if it is going to get attention and respect. Do not let it look as if it was an afterthought. Use bookstore fixtures. Don't furnish the bookstore with the cast-off and worn-out items that the library won't put in the public areas.

Do provide uniform and professionally created signage. Don't make it better than the library itself, but don't settle for less, either. The stakes are the same as in the library. Sooner or later, there will be pressure to sell some gift and stationery materials. Add inventory control to the obligations. There will be desire to create special promotional items for the library such as book bags and coffee mugs. Factor in the additional managerial and development cost.

FUTURE TRENDS

The good old annual book sale has a lot going for it, but consider it to be a harbinger of things to come. What is coming is a library used bookstore. Don't let it be forgotten in new building design, and even if a new building is not being planned, consider locating space for a bookstore in your present facilities. The nature of library browsing is going to change as public funding becomes more limited in public libraries. The presence of a bookstore is very comfortable for a lot of serious readers. Barnes and Noble or Borders probably will not replace the public library but smart librarians should pay attention to what they do there.

6 LEGAL RESOURCES IN THE PUBLIC LIBRARY

The community can be well served by having the county law library housed and maintained in the public library. Whatever opinions most Americans have about lawyers, it would be difficult to imagine this nation without the legal system. It would be equally difficult to imagine limited access to current legal information, and for that reason it would be desirable to have a working legal collection in the public library.

This is a nation based on law. If its citizens lack trust and faith in our laws, there can be no peace and order. The impact of this is never more apparent than when there are exceptional legal cases which are of nationwide interest. What would happen if there was no legal framework to rely on, one that the public trusted? The nation would be threatened, and fractured by dissent.

While the public is dependent upon the law, many are isolated from the legal system and the body of law. The average citizen relies on others to be aware of the law. This has evolved to the point where the average

person has little knowledge of what the law means. In part this is because legal information is inaccessible. Even the individuals confined in jails and prisons today have better access to the law than the average citizen. The courts have ruled that legal materials must be specifically available to inmates. Conversely, the average person outside of prison is unaware of his/her law library. Few have ever been to the courthouse library where all residents may have access to the law.

JUSTIFICATIONS FOR TRANSFERRING THE LAW LIBRARY

Access to the law has continued to be the primary purview of the lawyers and the legal community. The materials are extensive and generally some expertise is needed to use them well. Furthermore, the county law library may have limited hours of service, making legal resources less accessible to the general population.

Placement of the county law libraries into public libraries would accomplish several things which are in the long term interest of the community and the nation. It would remove the psychological barrier and "mystery" of the law, and eliminate the implication that legal information is limited to a special class of user. The law should be public information. Ownership, even though it was always available on some terms, is palpably in the hands of the general public. It would also put lawyers in more contact with other information sources. There is a great potential for symbiosis between the law and the rest of the world.

The other significant reason to consider a changed relationship pertains to quality. Please do not take these remarks out of context. There are many, many fine law libraries and their quality is not questioned. However, most communities do not have fine law libraries. Most communities, in fact, defer to the bar associations or judges to lead efforts to have any collective legal resources. Along with medicine, the law has been increasingly reserved to a professional cadre of practitioners.

Given the high cost of legal materials, it is next to impossible, other than for large communities or large law firms, to maintain significant law libraries. Many courthouses have relatively small collections of law books. Limited staffing and lax control render the small collections even less useful. Long-term borrowing may diminish the collection. There is no question that the primary users are the lawyers and the court employees. They are subject to the same temptations as the general public, given similar opportunity. The essential maintenance requirements of ordering, filing, classifying, shelving and monitoring are frequently honored in the breach. Public

libraries have infinitely more experience with such matters.

THE CASE FOR KEEPING THE LAW LIBRARY IN THE COURTHOUSE

There are also good arguments for not transferring the law library. Some will argue that the law library should remain in the courthouse because historically the collection's primary users have been in the courthouse. That is a questionable assumption today. As the law has become more and more complex, and its conduct has taken different directions, general legal research and courthouse legal activity have diverged. The former need no longer exists. Trial lawyers spend time in the courthouse, but it is generally spent in courtrooms and with other courthouse activity. Legal research is done in a law library (in-house or otherwise) or with online legal services. Further, it is done commonly by paralegal assistants and clerks other than the litigators. That is, the law library use is no longer directly connected to courthouse traffic.

The users of the library are increasingly less likely to combine research in immediate succession with a courtroom appearance. The lawyers do not have offices at the courthouse and a normal trip to the law library has no specific physical relationship to the courthouse. Legal personnel doing research are only incidentally going to or from the courthouse. In Orlando, Florida, the courthouse is across the street from the public library and there are relatively few joint visits.

Urban planners and managers with courthouse responsibility would probably see further benefit in moving the relatively passive activity of research from the often volatile action of jurors, trials, media, prisoners, bailiffs, etc.

PERSONNEL CONSIDERATIONS

Some will also say that law libraries need to have lawyers take care of the resources. This argument would have merit in a teaching law library and is easily understandable in the law library of a firm where a librarian is assisting in matters of interpretation. In a law library where the materials are maintained for the use of others, this is not the case. Legal materials are not any more challenging than many other public library resources. Public library staff members are quite competent to conduct the collection and maintenance functions of a law library. Experience may well serve better than no experience but that is no more problematic than any other new library service. Personnel changes occur in law libraries, too, and the ability to recruit and retain a librarian with knowledge of legal collections is more likely in a larger public library.

The value of conventional library applications are central to this question. Maintenance of resources and efficient, effective organization for general use is what public libraries do. They do it for many forms and formats of material. There is nothing about handling resources in law libraries that is not already being done in public libraries.

PHYSICAL FACILITIES

Another argument that may be voiced in favor of keeping the law library in the courthouse relates to the setting. Lawyers will perform better when the environment is conducive to their specialized work. Some of their research is confidential in nature. An environment created by lawyers or any

specialized group is likely to appeal to others of similar background. If the environment was being funded entirely by private means then the argument would be valid and a private design would be acceptable. However, if the law library is funded in some measure, if not completely, by public funds, than the nature and quality of the physical facilities should be in keeping with facilities designed to serve other identifiable portions of the community. That does not mean the facility would be lesser in scope or quality. Because the public library's mission is to ensure equitable service to the whole community, it can be expected to provide appropriate but equitable facilities for a law library.

Another argument in favor of retaining the law library in the courthouse is that the resources of a law library are different, requiring special knowledge. It simply isn't so. Legal terminology may be different, but the formats and suppliers are common to other portions of public library collections. While legal publishers may be different than science publishers, book jobbers can supply materials from any type of publisher regardless of the format or subject.

A further argument is that legal resources require more care and judgment. Every public library deals with resources which are used by different segments of the population. The propensity among the general population is to trust the librarians. Special interest users often feel that their particular interest needs more attention. If librarians give reasonably equal attention to legal needs as they give to medicine, education, video, fiction, repair, genealogy and all the others, then legal resources will probably get more proven attention than they are receiving at present.

COLLECTION DEVELOPMENT REQUIREMENTS

Some may argue that librarians will fail to buy appropriate materials for a legal services collection. As with other resources, librarians rely on qualified reviewers and recommendations from experts for much of their purchasing. I would expect that lawyers are able to articulate their needs at least as well as the rest of the population. The legal collection may benefit by receiving a broader range of recommendations in a public library setting, compared to a more specialized emphasis in the courthouse. The public librarian has no bias for any particular portion of the law, other than a desire for balance and a need to meet the community's present and future requirements.

INPUT FROM THE LEGAL COMMUNITY

A law library committee would be a reasonable device for maintaining a continuing dialog with the legal profession. A group of lawyers and judges, rotating seats on an advisory panel, could provide input to the public library staff to a degree commensurate to the interest of the legal community.

In the library of tomorrow, one needs to consider the form of the resources very carefully. There are a great many online legal services and CD-ROMs. This information can be easily searched, downloaded and transferred via telephone and cable lines and computer. There can also be some significant costs associated with these services. Ultimately such costs must have

public participation to insure that the legal collection and services do not become the province of a small minority of users.

In conclusion, there is nothing revolutionary about housing a law library in the public library. Lawyers would become more aware of library services, and may join other advocates for longer hours of access. Space away from high traffic is desirable for a legal collection, but this consideration is similar to planning for optimal service to other sectors of the community and the requirements of special collections. An integrated or separate catalog is a question which is rendered easier by automated techniques. Organizational considerations should include some specifically dedicated personnel, but local judgment must be the deciding factor because the size of the operations determine whether such skills are available.

Most of the roadblocks to placing law libraries in public libraries are political and emotional. Lawyers aren't any different from the rest of the public in the sense that they may resist change if they are uncertain of its impact, especially when their control and access to the legal collection are altered. Questions of costs and savings also may enter into consideration, although control and appearance of control are probably the prime motivators. Other logistical considerations could be central such as space, size, convenience, location or building codes. If conditions warrant consideration of a transfer of the law library to the public library, the change should be studied without emotion. There are logical reasons to support this consolidation, and an objective assessment should lead to the conclusion that it is in the best interest of the community.

7 BLACKWATCH: THE OVERNIGHT CREW

Public libraries conduct numerous repetitive tasks and some ponderous ones which can be conducted more efficiently when there are no conflicting priorities or physical traffic in the library. It's been my observation that a library crew, working the night shift, can accomplish more work than the same number of people working during public service hours.

As in any organization, the public library performs a number of routine activities for the benefit of its clientele. Libraries buy, prepare, and shelve books and other materials. They circulate them, answer questions, and perform a myriad variety of other related tasks for the benefit of the community. The individual employees who conduct these tasks are in unique position to see and test possibilities and variations of the simplest of acts and movements. There is, however, no particular reason to expect that each employee is going to assume the micromanagement of various units of the organization.

The managers, however, are charged with the responsibility of reviewing and analyzing the work and the work flow along with individual assignments. It is not an inherent skill. Some adapt well to it and can see relationships between tasks without much apparent effort. Most, however, must dedicate considerable effort to understand the personal interactions and the dynamics of work flow. Some people see and assimilate things differently than others.

For example, are we conducting operations during hours of user service which could be done with considerably more efficiency at a time when there is no conflict from the public or other priorities? This may sound easy but it isn't, for the entire environment of the library is now under discussion. To illustrate this, the Denver Public Library has operated its intralibrary delivery service primarily at night. Traffic is lighter, materials are more static, less gas is used, fewer staff are affected, there is less interruption, and all locations have more predictable pick up and delivery.

How significant are these factors? Somehow, all must be dealt with, either analytically or intuitively. Direct impacts are more obvious. Are employees available in sufficient numbers? Are there work rules that effect evening assignments? Are vehicles supported at night? Is access to locations clear and safe, and will the whole job be done with certainty?

Because there is such complexity, there is always an argument in favor of the status quo. It is usually the easiest solution. It doesn't improve anything, but it creates less anxiety and criticism. To be sure, it is sometimes the best course of action. Size is also a factor. There needs to be a significant amount of repetitive action in significant quantity for there to be the kind of savings which would justify such a change.

In a large circulation department there will be a constant flow of material being returned. Arguably much of this is popular material which other users want to borrow as soon as possible. Some of the materials will not be in high demand. Since staff cannot easily differentiate between the two, the solution is to get all of the books back on the shelves and to do it as quickly as possible.

Shelving books is problematic when the public is in the aisles, selecting and browsing. The book trucks partially block the aisles, and the shelvers cannot move about easily when users are in the way. Furthermore, shelvers should not interrupt users for the sake of restocking the shelves. Logic would dictate that staff can shelve more books when the public isn't present. There's less distraction, pausing or waiting, taking unnecessary time and motion. Of course, there are differences among shelvers, just are there are times during the day when shelving can be easily accomplished, and certain types of material need to be shelved as soon as possible.

In addition to returning books to the shelves there are many routine library tasks that could be more efficiently performed by staff during the hours the library is not open to the public. These include weeding, reference research, shifting books, mail preparation, moving collections, data entry, sorting, and shelf reading.

In Orlando, Florida, they called such a crew, Blackwatch (vigilance at night). Blackwatch is a night crew that keeps the workload even and prevents backups during the daytime shifts. The responsibilities are those selfless ones we tend to take for granted. It might be difficult to see the difference they make, unless you were in management or in an assignment where you had to worry about the ups and downs, the delays and the interruptions.

Every library has to deal with space reallocation, equipment transfers, and moving of resources. Frequently such moving causes confusion or safety concerns, and this requires closing the library to the public while adjustments are made. With a night crew such occasions can be minimized. The moving would be done at night and the daytime staff would be relieved of the potential disorder, anxiety and mess.

Review the routine work at your library and ask yourself if the public and staff are dealing with unnecessary obstruction and delay, which results in service reduction. It may involve fairly standard services, and routines that have been done for so long that no one even realizes any more that they interfere with good customer service. Of course, change could create problems, and there are those imponderable details. Let's consider what they might be.

MONEY

How can funds be found to reassign work to a night crew? Bear in mind that this work is already being done. Nothing new is being added. There may be a premium being paid for evening work, but this is more than offset by the greater efficiency. Reassignment of work to a night crew should really save money.

STAFFING

Where can the personnel be found? If the institution is large enough to consider a night operation, there are probably enough existing staff to implement this change. Many communities have commercial operations that run twenty-four hours a day. They are common and increasing in number. Another phenomenon in today's life-styles is that there are increasing numbers of people who, for their own private reasons, find it desirable to work nights. It may have to do with student schedules, child care or even another job.

Every organization has the ability to devise optional and attractive programs to attract volunteers for evening assignments from existing staff. If there is any relationship and trust, the odds are that reasonable solutions can be found. Consideration might be reduced hours, premium pay, promotion, increased vacation, regular schedule, fixed or flexible hours, reduced work pressure, preferred work assignments, parking, relaxed dress codes, among many others.

Changing work hours does have an impact on personnel. There will be differences in stamina and psychology among the employees who have opted for the night shift. Whatever the hours selected, there are some realities that can be expected. You will see some very tired people while they adjust their internal clocks. Changing the tasks and activities will be worth considering in order to maintain alertness.

FACILITIES

How can you operate a building all night long? For example, the building must be cleaned. In all probability much of the night work suggested could take place during hours when maintenance crews are also working in the building. It is quite possible that there will be no increase in the operating cost of the building. Air conditioning and heating are normally maintained through the night in order to avoid peaks and valleys or energy demand. Frequently buildings of any size have evening engineering staff for the purpose of monitoring the building systems, such as air conditioning, heating and pumps as well as fire control systems and computers of one sort or another. Building codes and standards usually require quite stringent controls for buildings of any size.

SERVICE

Does this really have an impact on service? The answer is in the nature of the library's use. If increasing numbers of citizens gain access to the library and its resources at less cost as a result of evening staff, it will definitely influence funding authorities. They will be more likely to support an efficiently managed public service, and that will sustain other portions of the budget for library materials and personnel.

There are few panaceas and there is no free lunch. The public libraries of this day and age are caught in the classic battle between the need to curtail costs and satisfying growing usage. One positive way to address these circumstances is to develop innovative ways of using staff more efficiently. If routine tasks can be shifted to personnel working a night schedule it can relieve some pressures on the public services staff. While every library will have to examine the complications of this change, it may offer rewards in terms of improved service and more efficient use of existing resources.

8 PALLETS, THE BIG EASY

Mental work is hard. Physical work is very hard. A little mental work can make the physical work much easier. The simple step of utilizing materials handling pallets in various library routines can improve public services. Moving and displaying materials on a pallet with a pallet jack saves a great deal of physical work and it can save time and improve accessibility and display.

Early in the history of the public library movement, when Andrew Carnegie's philanthropy was stimulating construction of many new library buildings, it was common architectural practice to design access with impressive stairways. This was primarily for aesthetic reasons, although in some instances it may have been justified by the nature of the site. At that time libraries had relatively few users browsing relatively small book collections. Handling books was not too difficult. Indeed, the library hardware of the day included those wonderful wooden book trucks. Unfortunately, they occasionally had to be lifted up and down stairs so they could be utilized on different levels. It didn't happen too often, thank goodness, for they were heavy. The manufacturers designed them with almost indestructible bearings. Some of them survive today and the moving parts often operate like new.

In the good old days, loading docks were also a different matter, if they existed. To be sure, there were far fewer books being published, delivered, processed, shelved and handled. In libraries today the equations have changed. The U.S. publishing industry generates 50,000–60,000 titles a year, and libraries try to buy as many as they can. Periodicals are an enormous business and libraries find them indispensable. The amount of energy used in moving periodicals in a library is a serious challenge today. Society has an insatiable need for more current information in a variety of formats. More services and information, of course, often means more paper to be moved and handled.

TAX FORMS

In the modern public library there is nothing quite like state and federal income tax forms. While there is controversy as to whether local libraries should furnish these forms, libraries are convenient for the taxpayers, and they are open longer hours. However wonderful this may be for the individual in need of the proper forms, it represents a problem for the library. In order to display and store dozens or hundreds of boxes of tax forms, something usually has to give. Space and handling are a real snag. Pallets are the answer, but many libraries cannot use them because of physical barriers in the building.

If the library can accommodate pallets, the formidable job of handling boxes of forms can be turned into a relatively simple process. The library shouldn't have any difficulty finding sources for pallet jacks and related hardware in the yellow pages. Once the equipment is available, staff can sort the boxes of forms onto pallets as they are removed from the truck. In many cases they will already be on pallets, which will further expedite processing. Moving a load of boxed forms with a pallet jack is much easier than handling the same load by hand. Ask the people who have to do the lifting.

If reasonable foresight is put into the arrangement of forms on the pallets, then the manual handling is finished. The pallets holding all the tax forms can be rolled to the temporary space in a public area. Preferably such space can be at or near the entry. Cut the tops off those boxes on the top of each stack and the display is complete. Someone will need to be assigned to monitor the display, discarding empty boxes and preparing new ones.

While moving materials may be challenged as to being directly involved with public service, it requires little imagination to see the relationship. If staff can handle materials faster, users will have quicker access.

Libraries with large amounts of incoming mail need to consider using mail handling carts and bins. These same libraries may receive books by the hundreds or thousands in a single shipment. Expediting handling will get new material to the shelves, where they will be accessible to the user. Shipments of that size normally will come off the shipping trucks on pallets. Those pallets should be rolled directly to the processing area by either the delivery firm or the receiving staff, depending on delivery terms and labor agreements. The same pallets should be handled at waist (working) level by the simple method of using another pallet handling device which raises the loaded pallet by means of a pneumatic jack.

IMPROVED BOOK PROCESSING

Using the proper equipment, even the smallest employee can safely handle a loaded pallet and raise it to an efficient working level. At this level a box of books can be opened and unloaded one book at a time or it can be pushed onto a table which is level with the box so others can process it. If acquisition and processing staff are prepared, four to twelve hours later the books can be available to the public. The speed, relative ease, and efficiency of processing new books can be greatly improved by utilizing the common pallet.

NEWSPAPERS AND MAGAZINES

How do libraries dispose of newspapers? Many libraries have a schedule for retaining and discarding newspapers. Many newspapers are now on microfilm and CD-ROM and online access is also popular. Their sheer bulk makes newspapers a likely target for elimination as alternative access becomes available. The same is true for magazines. As the retention schedules dictate, large quantities of newspapers and magazines must be removed from the public area. Put a pallet or two in the area and stack the discards on it. The pallet can be rolled away to the recycling area with little handling time or physical effort.

Have you ever seen a display of bestsellers in a bookstore or library? Some of them are formidable in size. Do you picture library staff creating the displays in the middle of the lobby? Are employees handling the books, moving them from place to place? Why not display those titles that are likely to quickly circulate using the pallet. Move them from a back room for instant display without any disruption as the change is made. Staff can be trained to prepare displays on a pallet with a minimum of effort.

APPEARANCE

Some may be critical that the pallet looks out of place in a public service area. Aesthetics may be a consideration, but necessity is the mother of invention and solutions will probably arise faster than they can be tested. For the most part, doing nothing is quite acceptable. There are very few people who are not familiar with pallets, and their function is obvious. A pallet in use is not offensive to most. Heavy fabric or oil cloth can be used to cover them, if desired. The fabric should be cut so it is larger than the pallet. Fold the ends to cover the pallet and staple or fasten the fabric to the pallet so it is completely covered. Put the cover on before loading the pallet with boxes. If the pallet is already full, wrap paper, cardboard, or cloth around it. The display will probably be temporary and excess attention is not warranted.

STAFF ACCEPTANCE

It's difficult to imagine a modern library that doesn't have many material handling problems and opportunities. Weeding, shifting, moving furniture and equipment, discarding, book sales, and other activities all provide the opportunity for pallets to save backs and time. A good gauge of how well pallets are accepted is to see how willingly the employees will return to the former procedure of lifting and handling boxes repeatedly from one end of the library to the other.

FACILITIES

Floor surfaces could become significant in the use of pallets. An occasional pallet jack rolling across the carpet doesn't seem to have any negative effect other than the fact that it won't roll as easy. Regular traffic lanes for pallet jacks should be tile or hard surfaces. This is important for both the employee and the surface. Since it is harder to move the jack on carpet, loads need to be lighter. Most carpet will be damaged sooner or later if it gets regular punishment from pallet jacks. The wise manager will also consider protection for sensitive corners. Wherever pallet jacks are used with any regularity, wall corners ought to be protected. Plastic or metal protective plates should be installed in appropriate places.

Pallets will save time and effort but nothing is perfect. Save the wall corners.

Doors are also worth mentioning. Sooner or later someone is going to try to get a pallet through a door without help. Depending on the direction relative to the hinges, the door is going to get scarred or damaged. Hardware is available to permit doors to be held open, and many libraries have already installed it for their book trucks. If it hasn't been previously installed, consider it for every door where pallet jacks are likely to be used.

Multiple jacks may be desirable depending on the volume of use. Sometimes two will be in use at the same time, or they will be used in locations that are far apart. In a large library there may be multiple buildings, such as remote storage, and that usually means more moving. In those circumstances, the library may wish to purchase a truck that will permit increased use of pallets.

This may appear expensive but never underestimate the cumulative cost of the employees who have to handle the materials, or the potential risk of injury or disability.

SOURCES OF PALLETS

Every metropolitan area has companies that make pallets. New pallets are more desirable than dirty ones. However, in the course of normal delivery and shipments to the library there will probably be a net surplus of pallets. Pull out the clean ones for use when it makes a difference. Libraries that acquire too many pallets can exercise a variety of different options. Destroying them is one alternative, but not a desirable one. A better choice is to recycle them through delivery companies that use them constantly in their own operations. Sometimes there is a market for them if they are an

Illustration 8.1: Pallet and pallet jack in use for book processing.

appropriate size and in good condition. Often, there are individuals and small businesses that will take them at no charge.

Size is a characteristic worth mentioning. If you have had no experience with pallets you may be surprised to find that the size, while fairly standard, is not universal. That is good and bad. Odd sizes don't always store easily. On the other hand, there may be some locations where you need a narrow pallet. Also, the industry is now making plastic pallets. Maybe the time is near when designer pallets will be available for locations where aesthetics are important. That could eliminate concerns about appearance while saving time and energy.

As tax support becomes more limited and public usage steadily increases, something has to give. If all avenues of improved efficiency and effectiveness are explored, one of them will be the use of pallets and pallet jacks. For handling large quantities of boxes this labor-saving technique will become a necessity. Adoption may require some initial investment, but the savings will be worth it.

POPULAR BOOKS

The phrase "popular books" refers to those public library books which a great many readers want to borrow. Providing users with what they want is what library service is all about. However, the issue of what to purchase for the library remains one of the major controversies in library service. Many of the individuals who played crucial roles in the development and formation of what we now call the public library were driven or guided in some measure by altruistic motives. They believed that there was intrinsic good in the availability of books for personal development. While they believed that they and their friends would benefit from this selection policy, they also believed it would be better for the community. It is unlikely that the early pioneers in the public library movement would have been active if they were not acutely interested in the value of books.

A second factor affecting the development of public library service, and possibly a more significant one, is that there were a limited number of books to select, relative to today. Choices had to be made about which books to acquire. Reading was not a universal capability. Language was diverse. For the relative few who were eager to read, almost any available book was probably worth reading. It is likely that users of these early, limited collections could say that they had actually read the majority of the available titles.

The early public libraries began in vastly different conditions than those of the library today. By the first half of the 20th century, conditions in the public library had changed enormously. There were so many more people in the American society. Publishing had profoundly increased. Libraries were everywhere, even in small communities. While public education was coming into its own, reading and leisure were not common. A relatively small number of people enjoyed and appreciated education more than most.

Most of them wanted education for all citizens. The altruism of this democratic ideal was pervasive. Compulsory education was achieved. All citizens could have a fair chance at success and personal satisfaction. In fact, it was required by law. Thus, competent and well intentioned fellow citizens would decide what was best for all.

We now have an education system that tries mightily to provide what is good and to do it for all citizens without regard to our differences. In this larger educational model, there exists a sense of how early library leaders may well have adopted and adapted library service and selection philosophy through the years. In the broad sense, our public libraries come from the tradition of commitment to education. The goals of education and fulfillment for our youth probably have more in common among taxpayers than any other single ambition.

Most parents want their children to be better off than they are, and the library has a role in achieving this goal.

The public library faces the ambiguous pull of regularized education for all as well as being the refuge of self-education and awareness. One is proscribed and the other is without boundaries. One is predominately for youth and the other makes no distinction.

As society has evolved, another fact has become quite clear. Portions of the community take care of their educational and informational needs apart from the public library. Academic libraries serve their student clientele and are oriented to a curriculum. School libraries are geared expressly for their K–12 audience. Special libraries with collections devoted to law and medicine cater to their specialized clientele. Private libraries serve special interests.

PUBLIC LIBRARY USERS

Who does the public library serve? Those involved in the public library movement would have you believe that it serves everybody. That may well appear in many public libraries' statements of purpose. The reality is that the public library cannot serve everybody equally. Of course, everybody is free to use it. Individuals who use the specialized libraries may also use the public library. The converse is not generally true. There are some who would use the public library for the same purpose that they use the special one. The extent to which they are successful is a reflection on the relative quality of libraries. Can the public library maintain resources for all specialized groups? It is unlikely.

The public library may attempt to serve special groups with limited resources and competence in those specialties, but it lacks the funding to be successful. In the current governmental funding environment it is very unlikely that there will be a transformation. The public library will continue to be available for all to use as they can. The inescapable truth is that large proportions of the community enjoy other publicly funded library services and resources.

The public library's general users are those who do not have alternative sources of information. The public library cannot be the major library resource for the college student in the field of philosophy. That student is in a controlled environment and the college provides material for that particular curriculum. The medical practitioner's major source for material on medicine is the medical library.

That leaves the public library with the responsibility to serve a vast unaffiliated group of citizens, and what do they want and need? The general public does not ask much of the public library. Nonetheless, individuals sometimes make a fuss. Sometimes a number of individuals make a fuss at the same time. The public library perceives itself as so responsive that it tries to respond to individuals as if they were thousands of protesters at the front door, clamoring for satisfaction. Considering how respectful, courteous and sensitive librarians are, such response is altogether laudable. Librarians just do not like squeaky wheels and everyone seems to be happier when they try to help.

When there are repeated requests for the same books and when our own data demonstrates that hundreds of citizens want to read the same books, what should we do? Keep in mind that the public library is the only source these taxpayers, the general public, have to get the book. Invariably, the public library takes the position that it can only do so much about popular books.

BIAS IN POPULAR BOOK SELECTION

Popular books frequently are not purchased in quantity because of criticism regarding the quality of the writing. There are other justifications if they are needed. The library cannot buy every book, therefore it cannot buy multiples of one at the expense of others. Fiscal restraints cause us to limit the number of copies. There are other rationalizations, most librarians have used them.

The citizen is never told that the library has decided that "it would be better for you and your children if we purchased books which would be more valuable in the future than books which you wish to read now."

It is hard to resist the notion that the successful user, the satisfied taxpayer, is the one who asks something of the library and it is provided. Already having determined that the general public is the group with primary claims on the public library, the optimum service is that service which meets the need of the general public.

USER SATISFACTION

Public libraries should buy what the taxpaying public wants to read. There are boundaries of taste and quality which will test the selection skills. In the main, popular books such as bestsellers should be purchased in quantity commensurate with user interest. As for the other types of books in the collection, there is little doubt that the public will ask for them as well.

For the interested users, there are few services the public library can provide which provides as much satisfaction as a bestseller at the time the user wants to read it. It is not the library's role to judge the public interest. Multiple copies do not consume the entire book budget. Successful service usually means improved funding albeit an immediate impact would not be a realistic expectation. Change takes time. Happy people are better to deal with than unhappy people.

BENEFITS OF BUYING MULTIPLE COPIES

Keep in mind that when a book budget allocates proportionately more money on popular books there are likely to be some unexpected opportunities. Every librarian is familiar with *Roots* by Alex Haley. The public library in Orlando, Florida, bought 500 copies in the 1970s. The title received heavy use and then natural attrition permitted the library to avoid buying replacement copies for almost 20 years. The original copies cost $12.50 list. That has to be viewed as a good investment.

When a library begins to process significant quantities of the same title, one curiosity is the impact on processing time. All of those identical books must mean that processing can be handled at its highest efficiency. For example, what marking do you put on the book? Libraries have carried book processing procedures and standards forward through the decades. In fact, processing of multiple copies of bestsellers can be greatly simplified.

Think of a public library where there is always a selection of current bestsellers. Imagine a display where users can find just what they want without searching. Imagine a section of new books that are really new. The library staff would also be confronted with change. If the promised books were available, accountability would be close at hand.

An untested option of multiple copies is to make the supernumerary copies available to other libraries. Inevitably there will be copies of some titles that could be dis-carded. A used bookstore is one possibility, but a better possibility is other public libraries. Since most libraries are victims of traditional book selection policies, most of them have sizable waiting lists for popular books long after our aggressive library's taxpayers have been satisfied. Most libraries, in the meantime, are replacing and adding copies of popular titles and doing it with some regularity.

Special display possibilities are endless for large numbers of the same title. Libraries have trained the users to know that bestsellers are seldom available in quantities to satisfy need. There are plenty of users who reserve a popular book without looking for it because it would be so unusual to find one on the shelf. There are former users who have given up on the public library because it does not have sufficient numbers of popular books. Imagine, on the other hand, their enthusiasm if they could have a reasonable expectation of finding popular titles at any time in the library.

Why, decades of mind sets would begin changing. Such adjustment in no way suggests that other aspects of the library program would suffer. Proportionately, one would find that a segment of the general public would use the library more often than they had in the past. There is nothing wrong with that. The public library can survive the popular book paradigm and do so to its own enhancement.

REFERENCE SERVICE

Much of the inefficiency of reference work is not evident in the various components of the process. The inefficiency in reference work is due largely to the way in which libraries have collectively executed the various tasks. The public library could significantly improve reference service by reorganizing the methodology of assigning and completing the various tasks involved in reference work.

While most, if not all, of the following suggested ideas have been tried and implemented at the Orange County Library System, it is important to keep in mind that the various items are separately executed. That is, rather than isolating the components or aspects of reference and dealing with them one by one, the challenge is to confront the entire scope of reference activity for the purpose of improving the efficiency and effectiveness of the service. The library must examine the purpose as well as the process. What is being done and why?

Much of what is done in reference work is based on traditionally accepted procedures. Consider that the library comes from an academic tradition. The clientele to be served was made up of students and their handlers, the teachers. The emphasis of reference work was inwardly directed. That is, the questions and the assistance was primarily devoted toward an academic discipline. Learning, sharing, and collecting the literature were the primary objectives. The public library, as it developed, evolved into an institution with different reference objectives. The public library's clientele consisted of a wide cross section of the public. It is not from a limited group of any kind. The questions and inquiries come from every age group, and they have no limitation as in a fixed curriculum. They come from the breadth of the society.

THE LIBRARY'S CHANGING ROLE

Public library reference work has been changing through the years. It has become more diverse, reflecting the varied interests of the public. That has directly affected the public library, which has had some difficulty defining its mission. It has taken on all comers and looked for more. The public library has adopted a philosophy that we serve all who come to us. It is a goal that has increasingly become more difficult to fulfill. While the library's reference role and expectations have grown, the methodology of conducting the service has stayed essentially the same. The content and diversity of the public inquiries and demands have changed dramatically, but the way the service is provided has stayed largely the same. Yet the funding has kept pace with growth. Through the decades, public library funding stability has kept libraries operating, large ones and small ones, year in and year out. The reality that public libraries must now begin facing is that funding sources will not continue to provide dollars for libraries in the same measure as in the past.

Individual libraries have faced the threat. Some have closed, temporarily it is hoped. Most have considered the fact that funding is limited, and resigned themselves to it, assuming that little can be done. How is reference service responding to the new reality? Some believe that technology will save the day, and others believe that everybody gets some bad luck sooner or later. There is not enough introspection to determine whether some of the problems and solutions exist within the library walls. We have been fortunate that the public is traditionally on the side of the library, but that may change. Those libraries that look at the expenses associated with reference service and find ways to hold the line on costs may enjoy and deserve the public's continued support.

What is meant by the reference process? It is all of the steps employed by the library staff in the satisfaction of a customer's request for information. The processes which are employed by the library and librarians represent the cost centers as well as the effectiveness of the response. Operating hours, switchboards, phone systems, physical layout, staffing, technology, management and support are also cost components. These are all used but may be beyond the immediate scope of this discussion. Instead, this discussion is directed toward the basic procedures and steps of conducting reference service.

REFERENCE PERSONNEL

Staff is the most expensive element, the most sensitive and the most enduring of the library costs. The staffing process, therefore, is the most significant of the cost centers to examine. To understand the personnel skills required in reference service, examine the types of inquiries that fall under the rubric of reference. Look at them generally in the context of any public library's effort. Sample reference questions include: Find books on a subject. Provide the correct spelling of a word. Hold certain videos for pick-up. Do you have a specific title? If so, mail it to me. Can you tell me when a dignitary died? Do you have words to a certain song? What is the fair market value of my car? I need books to help with teaching a school lesson. What companies make widgets? What is the phone number and address of a specific company. Do you have a specific handbook or test manual? How do you say hello in French? Do you have a specific magazine article? When was the ADA passed? Who lives at this address?

What time is it in London? And on and on, ad infinitum.

To respond to this variety of questions requires different skills and responses from the librarians. These responses are always individual–one on one. Furthermore, the information that is provided seems to be adequate. The problem with the through-put of the work is not the competencies of the reference staff but other aspects of the process.

RESERVE PROCEDURES

Consider reserves. Reserving books is a repetitive task that normally requires little more than completion of a form. The task is improved substantially by an awareness of authors and titles. Support staff is perfectly capable of conducting the great majority of these bibliographic reserve inquiries. Why not locate the reserves function away from the reference desk. There will be some logistical or staffing problems to overcome, but the significant change will be in the reference service. Depending on the traffic, a healthy measure of work will be released from the reference librarians. If a supporting staff member has an inquiry which is beyond the resources at hand, it can be quite routine to shunt the question to another location, namely to a librarian. It should also be possible to use technology to improve the reserves process. Save the most demanding tasks for those best trained to meet the challenges.

SUBJECT INQUIRIES

Take subject requests. It should be possible to move the responsibility to lower paid staff to help those users seeking books "on" or books "about" a subject. That part of the work which is straightforward is as easily accomplished by the support staff as a librarian, and it provides the support staff with more variety and challenge. In some cases the most difficult and time consuming portion of filling subject requests is the travel time spent in traversing the distance between a service point and the bookstacks where the subject is located. To be sure, there is much library lore concerning the potential of simple requests actually becoming sophisticated research questions. The reality is that normally the question is the question, and a book that addresses a user's need for information on a subject fills the bill. The better the collection, the easier this becomes, as all librarians know.

TELEPHONE REFERENCE SERVICE

Focusing the activities of the most expensive staff will permit more creative and efficient use of all the staff. Consider the telephones. Many libraries offer a telephone reference service. Removing the phone calls from the reference desks will improve stability and coherence. Frequently the solution to a problem is in part the resolution of a symptom. The symptom is that the interrupting and out-of-sequence phone calls are frequently very disruptive at the reference desks. Removal of most of the phone calls clearly reduces the competition at the desks.

Does it solve the basic problems? Frequently not. Just because the phone calls are reduced does not mean that the quality of the responses is improved or that the process has become more efficient with the library resources. If the staff at telephone reference is not as skilled as the staff at the reference desks, the quality of the phone service may suffer. If the same staff is being spread to the telephones in a different location, it may be that the pressures and frustrations are merely exchanged for another set. Moving among schedules may seem easier for librarians but it may be inefficient. Nevertheless, a reassignment of telephone reference service to support staff might improve the efficiency of the service, and maintain quality if adequate training is provided, and referral to professional staff is arranged for more difficult questions.

As with many innovations and changes, appearances can be deceiving. All examinations go back to the original question. What is the library's mission? What are the goals of the reference service? The responses to these questions may sometimes be revealing. If the library is doing things which are not included in the goals, there is the potential of some quick adjustment. Eliminate those activities which are outside of the library's mission. If an area of concern stems from the presence of ambiguous policies, then clarification can smooth the waters.

STATISTICS

Much of the knowledge of what we do comes from librarian-generated statistics. Unfortunately, libraries do not have in place the data collection components of management which foretell usage and gauge public response to new services. Libraries may have done quite well in the past without such tools but that will not be possible in the future. The major salvation of the public library may well rest with the technology that is used in reference work. Libraries must know how their dollars are being spent. In terms of reference service,

the largest cost center in the library, we are unlikely to solve its vexing problems until the underlying premises are proven. In short, the public library staff must know the precise nature of reference work on a daily basis. Further, the staff must know how the inquiries were handled and if appropriate responses were given. The only way such data can be collected in a way to reveal the needed information is to improve data collection.

An earlier chapter (Greeter) portrayed one method of examining reference success by collecting data on directional questions. That effort, while useful and illuminating, concentrated primarily on just one type of question. The results may be useful but it does not reveal the institutional process of reference work. What happens when the reference staff is confronted with questions they cannot answer? A great many libraries opt for the distressingly simple conclusion to limit the amount of time that will be spent on any single question. It works for most. One major library limits the time to answer a single question to three minutes. Staff answers 600 questions per day, and another 2,000 calls don't even get through. That scenario comes directly from the public library tradition. Something must be done about it. The library is as comfortable as most organizations in the application and usages of computers and computer technology. It needs to apply the wonders of computers to the traditionally executed service of reference assistance. Just as librarians instantaneously know the disposition of an item in circulation, they need to know everything about reference transactions. After all, the reference transaction is considerably more expensive.

The great circular discussions about reference are usually predicated upon sampled, experiential and anecdotal data supplied by the subjects of the discussion, the reference librarians. They are acknowledged to be under pressure and beset from all sides by users of every description while they are armed with policies which frequently beg logical distinctions. This is hardly the environment in which to collect the impersonal data required to sort out effectiveness and efficiency on the reference desks. If librarians believe in the value of the technology, there will be a dramatic turn toward computerizing and analyzing the reference process. Data from these programs will permit librarians and institutions to see specifically and continuously the dynamics of their reference service. Absorbing such data, librarians will be able to make informed judgements about the numbers and scope of reference service.

This information will lead to separation of the various types of reference and insight which will lead to the development of procedures which can add efficiency to reference work. Quality needn't suffer. On the contrary, as the various parts of reference are done with more focus, quality will improve. As quality improves, the major studies of public library reference work will finally begin to show that most questions can indeed be answered correctly.

The most valuable basis for an automated process is the clear knowledge of what already exists. Exactly what is it that one wishes to automate? Studies and diaries take on a new importance, especially if they contain knowledge and insight into the process of reference. It is the process that librarians employ which will yield the necessary information. When a patron approaches or a call in received, what happens? When a librarian is interrupted, how is the problem handled? If a caller is put on hold, how is the caller retrieved? Is there any record of the specific question? Is the answer methodically recorded? How is a question transferred between departments and other agencies? What exactly does a librarian do with a reserve? Where and how are titles verified? How and when does a librarian cease pursuing a question? How and when does a manager become involved in reference work? Most librarians could easily expand this list. Note that it is not the librarian skills which are at the heart of the problem. It is the process. The process has changed in the face of ever changing public demands. The changes in the process have been largely small and subtle but they have been many.

The results of the changes have brought reference service almost to the brink of functional gridlock. Librarians have learned to say yes to most entreaties and in doing so have created a conglomeration of efforts and responses which defy logical execution. That is why libraries must turn to technology for a solution to the problem. I believe that once we understand the real nature of the public's information needs and our responses, we will develop a new range of more specialized services.

FUTURE REFERENCE SERVICE

One such breakdown would be as follows:

Bibline: Bibliographic questions and reserves handled by a support cadre.

First Interface: Hours, services, referrals, instant answers (i.e., CPI).

Answer Librarians: Who don't even face the public but spend their uninterrupted time answering questions.

Reader's Guidance Librarians: providing the interface to all walk-in users whether they want fiction or nonfiction material.

This hypothetical organization does not remove librarians from the essence of reference work. It does change the process and alters the handling of the various components of the work, departing dramatically from the traditional norms.

Central to the execution of this unfamiliar reference work is the computer. Without the online storage and instantaneous, remote interaction capabilities of the computer it would not be possible. Also significant is the new capability of maintaining the entire work effort online, whether for service, strategic or tactical planning, creation of new data bases, reporting or evaluation. One can know with relative ease the precise status of the service. How are these computer components accommodated? The basic reference process database and programs are stored and utilized on a computer.

At the Orange County Library System, where this concept has been tested, network software presently supports 100 stations. The reference software includes twenty screens for various functions. In addition to the reference software, other databases on hard disk or on CD-ROM products are supplied to the network. Both PCs and terminals are in use on the network. Ten or twenty stations have telephone headsets for simultaneous phone use with keyboards while engaged with the public. Bibline, reference desks, phone interview-

ing, answer librarians and subject retrievers are in different physical locations but connected by the reference computer network and programs.

The integration of various components of reference service which operate in different locations puts teamwork into practice. While it is normal in libraries to rely on a proclamation of teamwork to get the job done, this scheme requires that the different portions of the team execute parts of the job physically separate and independent of one another. Members of the team may well not see each other in a week although they are working together on the same questions and for the same users.

As the service of the library becomes more integrated, there are happy coincidences. The chapter on Books By Mail points out some of the benefits of receiving books at your mailbox. It is possible through the USPS to achieve next day delivery of packages of books. Marrying next day delivery to streamlined reference selection, coupled with evening pick-up of mail, means that a user can call in the afternoon to ask for books about a specific subject and receive them in the mail the very next morning. Now, who would make a special trip to save a few hours? The truth is that libraries have a notoriously poor success rate on holding books for the users to come by and pick them up.

In conclusion, effective reference service in the future will depend on better knowledge of user needs and staff response, adoption of new technology, realignment of staff assignments, and a willingness to consider change.

11 REFERENCE RUNNER

Public librarians who are in reference services are usually involved in many clerical, repetitive tasks. Many of them are under-performing in these assignments, and this is an unacceptable waste of public funds. If given a choice, most librarians would opt for continuous professional tasks. The solution is another type of position that would free librarians from paraprofessional work. A "reference runner" at a lower pay classification in reference service could handle many of the routine tasks, resulting in a lower cost to the taxpayer and a reasonable expectation of better results.

There are some aspects of reference work which are handled by librarians because no one else is available to do them. There are locations where the librarian is the sole employee available. There may be times of the day or of a shift when the same is true even in a larger library. In the same fashion there are occasions when support staff have to perform clerical functions. In many public libraries across the nation, there are significant numbers of staff who perform professional duties but lack professional education. It is a reality that must be acknowledged.

The building must be checked, the cards must be filed, the data must be entered, books must be plated, users must be directed to the restroom, materials must be picked up from the tables, the spill must be cleaned up, and life must go on. Depending on circumstances, whoever is present should take care of the routines. If, however, the only person around is the reference librarian, who will do them?

Economics will affect the answer. One standard will assume that the librarian is reserved for the professional work and that such routines are not appropriate tasks for the librarian. Every librarian, however, knows that it is vital for such routines to be kept up. The librarian will begin performing clerical tasks out of service-driven instincts and needs. The librarian may sometimes conduct the tasks because they are preferable to non-stop public interface.

Maybe just getting off your feet for a while is the justification.

In any case, it is in the interest of the taxpayer that, over time, (a) library staff is utilized productively and that (b) the utilization is efficient in the interest of cost. These are universal observations and almost beg the question.

DEFINING PROFESSIONAL WORK

Are the librarians on the staff performing more clerical work or are the clerical employees performing more professional work? The ratio is the key but understanding the mix and the roles is fundamental. A choice is present and it has a philosophical origin. What is professional reference work and what is not? It is certain that some of our large libraries confront the question routinely. In some of these libraries there are negotiated agreements that a professional degree is necessary before an employee can undertake reference service. There are others where only paraprofessional staff accept and screen phone calls to assess whether referral should be made to the professional staff. These procedures are carefully developed by serious, dedicated and honorable people at different levels who have professional insight into the public's information needs.

For the most part, the world believes that the person they contact at the reference desk is a reference librarian, even though that may not be correct. Of course, some users are aware of the difference in training and or background. Most users are not. Their relationship to the information and help is the same, regardless of the provider. If it's good, they like it and if it's bad, they don't like it.

Librarians often think the public can tell the differences between services provided by paraprofessional and professional staff. Clerical staff often think there is no difference at all. The user is after help with library resources and the primary evaluative judgment is whether or not they get it. Seldom does anybody ever ask if they got it from a librarian or a clerk. Frankly, the people who care and to whom it matters are the stakeholders who relate directly to the jobs, the employees and managers. The qualitative differences are likely to be more interesting from librarian to librarian than between librarians and non-librarians.

The entire issue is one that has had attention by the library profession for longer than the library degree has existed. There are differences between librarian roles in public, academic, school and special libraries. Some other professions have distinctly different methods and environments which makes the distinction easier. What is important in reference work is not who performs the service, but whether the public receives accurate, prompt service, at reasonable cost to the taxpayer. In many instances, a paraprofessional "reference runner" may be able to best satisfy those requirements.

The future of the public library is not an absolute. Nothing is permanent. In the sweep of civilization, library degrees have been around for a very brief time. There is a valid place for them, but there is a danger in the presumption that library degrees are indispensable in the public library regardless of the size of the institution.

Money and how it is spent is the underpinning of a tax supported agency. The best service for the least money is a fair generalization, at least for a typical government service. There are other variables but none as stark as that one. If one can buy a service for a dollar, why would one pay more? The trouble with assessing reference service is that there is no general agreement within the profession on how to assess the quality of the service. There is an alternative way to resolve this problem.

If portions of the service are handled by paraprofessionals, the service should be tested from the perspective of the buyer, the taxpayer.

QUALIFICATIONS

If reference runners are employed to provide some levels of reference service, what qualifications are required? Furthermore, should they be at a substantially lower pay classification? Does a reference runner need a bachelor's degree? Can clerical staff be employed in this assignment? There are probably many employees who are intellectually and emotionally capable of performing portions of the reference work. If you consider any large group of library clerks you will find a variety of strengths. Some clerks are students, already possessing the education and maturation to perform public service reference work. Some are working people without ambition other than to be employed in interesting work. Others may be quite capable of high level work but have never had the opportunity. By the same token, many employees lack the personal characteristics as well as the education, maturity or stability to take on higher commitments. There are people who can and would respond well to increased responsibility and challenge.

Why is it that libraries are unwilling or unable to develop personnel classifications and duties which maximize personal growth in such a way? Probably it is related to status and job security, not unlike other groups which protect their members. If service is the question, then it can be demonstrated that well chosen individuals can perform all of the marginal duties of a librarian and some of the more sophisticated ones as well.

The library profession has for years acknowledged the desirability of upward mobility, of career ladders. What more valuable employee is there than the long term employee who has roots and loyalties to an organization that has been responsive and responsible? Personnel choices at all levels should receive the maximum care and concern. There are characteristics that turn out to be more vital than the possession of degrees.

ROLES FOR THE REFERENCE RUNNER

Having addressed concerns about the qualifications of the reference runner, what about their specific role in reference service? Books, books, books and more books are the underpinnings of reference service. In addition, books are being supplanted with magazines, brochures, microfilm, CD-ROM, computers and electronic data transfer. As a rule, the person who works with books and titles constantly has a better working knowledge of them than the person who doesn't. Librarians have filled out reserve requests until they are blue in the face. The justification is that a librarian has a better knowledge of books and bibliographic research. The runner, therefore, would require a similar knowledge.

Computers, computers, computers are increasingly becoming the tools of every trade. Data entry and computer operation are not professional reference skills. They may be done by librarians but there is every reason to believe that this could be done more effectively by clerical staff. Most young people have been weaned on computers. Those who are already on the job have been converted.

There should be general agreement that directional questions could be effectively handled by the reference runner. Building and operating facts can be dispensed as easily and at a cheaper cost by clerks rather than by librarians. However, directions to another portion of the collection could benefit from working knowledge of specific resources. Experience, on the other hand, says that familiarity with the library will teach the sources, the degree process does not.

There was a time when bibliographic expertise was a stronger factor in the librarians' bag of skills. That has been mitigated and diminished by changes in publishing and in access tools. The magnificent tools available today make bibliographic work very simple. Communication by the users is so pervasive that the library may by challenged more by queries that lack precision than by those which are elusive because of the limitations of the sources. The good librarians knew the sources in the old days but the improvement of the sources has rendered that a questionable advantage.

Reference librarians are not under attack here. The use of their skills to satisfy simple questions is in question because of their higher salaries. Each routine task that a reference runner can assume to relieve the librarian should represent improved effectiveness for the librarian. Maintenance of a desirable mix of staff is in everyone's interest. To the extent that a runner is perceived as a threat, the library will remain inefficient.

LIBRARIAN BURNOUT

There are a couple of other overarching factors that deserve mention. Institutional organization and expectations change over time and sometimes foster apathy or lethargy. Librarians who have been doing the same jobs for years may get into a rut. Unfortunately, some managers have a tendency to go along with these lapses. Loss of excitement, drive, enthusiasm, enjoyment, confidence, belief or most anything can be insidious and show up over time as a general malaise. The reference desk might be considered as the end of someone's career. A significant motivator is now missing if there are no more rungs on an individual's career ladder.

Another factor is the nine-to-five syndrome. Many of us are in positions of fiscal necessity. We are working because we feel that it is necessary for the revenue and not because there are any other emotional attachments. If there is no more motivation to work in the library than at any other place, then the result will be less than sterling.

Our routine decisions are often based on superficial stimuli. The concept of the reference runner is based on the premise that we are not always thinking about the most important ingredients of the workforce or how it is molded. With regard to reference service, we can accomplish at least the same goals and probably more. We can do it at a lower cost per user contact and we can build in rewards and satisfaction. Each library must design the roles. There are no universal rules for this position. The future of reference service deserves whatever organizational efforts we can expend.

12 DRIVE-UP WINDOW

DRIVE-UP WINDOW

Library drive-up windows have been around for a long time. Even walk-up windows are not a new idea. Nonetheless, libraries that have drive-up windows are in a small minority. They exist because they can improve user accessibility and convenience to the library. Indeed, some libraries have procedures that allow users to call ahead and arrange to pick up material at the drive-up window without going inside. Most of the use at present is for the conventional and simple return of books. It saves time, avoids the necessity for the user to come into the library, and if parking is at a premium, the user doesn't have to search for a place to park.

To the extent that the window is in continuous use, it may also be of considerable benefit to the library. Some windows may have traffic of over 7,000 cars a month. That saves wear and tear on equipment, carpet and doors. Users are more likely to return materials on time, avoiding the expense of contacting them. Earlier return increases

the use of library materials. Some of these savings are marginal, but they are real, nonetheless.

SOCIETAL TRENDS

Assuming that mobility will continue to be important in our society, there are likely to be more and more cars and drivers in most communities, and therefore the pool of potential users will be larger. Business trends will also have an impact on the acceptability of the drive-up window.

Banks, automated teller machines, ice cream stands, fast food restaurants, photo processors, dry cleaners, churches, and many other services offer drive-up windows. The idea isn't unusual in society today. What is unusual is the limited use of the drive-up window among public libraries.

The variety of services available through the window ultimately will have the greatest impact on the success of this feature. Consider what the library offers—books, including other formats of materials, and it provides information. As yet, there is negligible mailing of materials. Virtually the only way users can get library books is to come into our institutions and check them out. In spite of numerous small scale exceptions, this is not an enviable record for a public institution which has been around for a hundred years. Surely we can offer something that would be of greater benefit and convenience to the user.

PACKAGED SELECTIONS

There are many individuals and families with life-styles that do not have the opportunity for regular trips to the library. Some of these individuals are readers who would enjoy the library. They just cannot visit the library because of the library's hours or other barriers. For example, the parent of young children may love to read but cannot visit the library because of the cost and/or difficulty of finding a sitter. Bringing very young children into the library may be difficult, or the parent may not have the time to get the children dressed and ready to visit the library. But what if this parent could go to a drive-up window and check out a package of books? Wouldn't this fulfill some of the family's reading needs? What if someone could also check out a prepackaged set of books for the preschoolers in the family?

Prepackaged sounds like a bad word in this business, but in this instance it could consist of a collection of classic and standard recreational reading. If the selections are not appropriate, the packages will not succeed. For example, there are children's titles which are almost never available because they are out in circulation. Why not buy and put these books into packages so a harried mother or father could pick them up while on an errand.

Virtually every store puts ads in their windows. The drive-up window should have books displayed, however few, so that a driver could pick something up on impulse. Remember that many of these individuals are not going to come into the library under any circumstances, because don't have the time.

What if the library had several different generic sets of books available, and they were available at numerous drive-up locations in the community? By generic sets, I mean several books with common interest or focus. Several books on retirement, business, investing or careers might well strike a chord with many users. What if the library had other sets of mysteries, science fiction, or other types of material that were prepackaged and available from drive-up locations? How about five or ten books by the same fiction author that could be checked out for nine or twelve weeks?

SERVICE HOURS

Expanding the hours of access to library service by increasing hours of a drive-up window might attract more users. Some people simply cannot go to the library because of their work hours or family obligations. Limiting the additional service to that which can be provided via the drive-up window might make such a change fiscally feasible. Why not be open all night with limited service? Why not let the public call anytime they wish? Of course it may require advance warning to get a book from another collection and to lend it from the window, but that is a procedure that can be addressed.

Learning what our citizens want and need may be more complicated than we realize. Asking them whether they want library service twenty-four hours a day may not be very useful if they've never experienced it. However, once they see and use it, they may prefer it to more traditional service.

It has been my experience that 5,000 to 7,000 drivers a month will use a convenient drive-up window at a busy library. Their immediate user purpose may be primarily to return books, but there is a real danger to us if we underestimate the importance of convenience. Maybe they saved ten minutes or an hour. Maybe there was no available parking. Maybe there is some physical impediment that makes the drive-up window preferable today. Maybe the books are heavy or ungainly. Whatever the motivation, it is clearly an important factor that will affect an individual's library use.

ECONOMIC JUSTIFICATIONS

Some may question how it is possible to justify such an expense on the basis of convenience. There are other savings that might not be readily evident. For example, what does a parking place cost in your community? Ask your city or county planner. How long does it take a citizen to park a car, navigate to the door of the library, deal with the physical arrangement and then turn around and do it all over again? It is not insignificant time for an individual if he/she has something else to do. How much does it cost the institution to provide the basic facility? Be cautious about asking this question because the answer is problematic for the non-users. How much heat or air conditioning is lost when thousands of individuals open the doors of the building?

Conversely, how much does it cost to staff a window? Is that staffing which would not be needed inside? This may be a question that is determined by the library's priorities.

There are many management questions to ponder when a drive-up window is under study. However, libraries are service organizations, and librarians exist to provide service to the users. I believe it is safe to say that a great many users will find it desirable to use a drive-up window. If funds are limited, users would say that you should eliminate another service that is not as heavily used.

DESIGN ELEMENTS

If a library does decide to install a drive-up window, don't overlook any of the following planning and design factors:

- Provide one way traffic access to the driver's side of the car.
- Provide an immediate car approach environment for safe driving.
- Allow room for some car queuing behind the car at the window
- Ensure that the height of the drawer is equal to the height of the car window.
- Ensure that the height of the library work station is equal to the height of the driver.
- Before selecting the drawer or window-opening assembly test the physical ease of operation.
- Check the size of the drawer or opening relative to maximum activity expected in the location.

Illustration 12. 1: Library
drive-up windows need
careful design to ensure
they are efficient for
users and staff.

- Decide whether a drawer is actually needed compared to a window.

- Based on local climatic conditions, decide whether to have protection overhead for sun or rain.

- Determine the window's exposure relative to sun angle or reflection from other source, and plan on needed window treatment.

- Based on anticipated traffic and the volume of materials to be moved through the window, estimate the amount of space that will be required.

- Discuss the desired visibility and lighting for the window with your architect.

- Determine whether amplified communication between staff and driver will be needed.

- Determine whether the staff at the window will need access to library records for circulation.

Illustration 12.2: Drive-up windows can attract customers who lack time for traditional library service.

- Determine what book return capabilities will be required, including a cash register, change, receipts, etc.

- Determine what physical relationship will be needed between the window and the circulation department.

- Decide on the degree of ease that will be needed in moving materials to and from the window.

- Consider the physical comfort of staff assigned to the window.

Drive-up service has been proven in many businesses and public library settings. It's time that more public libraries recognized that we now live in a very mobile society, and drive-up access will benefit users and increase usage.

13 BOOKS BY MAIL

The most underutilized method of bringing users and library books into contact with each other is by the United States Postal Service (USPS). Public libraries generally have overlooked or rejected the alternative of mailing large quantities of books directly to their users.

There are several reasons for this. One common measure of a library's success is walk-in traffic. If 20,000 books were mailed per month, how many individuals do not have to come to the library at all? However, if we re-examine the purpose and goals of library service, it is to provide users with convenient access to information and resources. If that can be more efficiently accomplished by mailing books to users, then bringing them into the library should not be quite as significant as we imagine, especially if it reduces the user's transportation and logistical requirements.

Many medium and large public libraries mail books to shut-ins. Effective procedures have been devised and are being used. It is merely an extension in scope to increase the numbers. Indeed, many of the shut-in services are already called something like "books-by-mail." Two larger libraries, King County, Washington, and Orange County, Florida, have been mailing tens of thousands of books per month for many years. A recent and dramatic postage increase signaled a curtailment at King County Library. Orange County continues to mail books at a rate of over 20,000 per month, a number which is increasing.

Sending books through the USPS is not a wild and crazy thing. Other libraries have done so and some are still doing it, although it is usually in very small quantities. To advance the notion that large quantities of books could be mailed, however, creates uncertainty. A number of objections may be raised: It's different, it's expensive, it's untried, it's difficult, it's without sponsors, etc. It has also been done for twenty years. Virtually any format, but mostly books, are being mailed. Many libraries offering books by mail place no eligibility restriction based upon the users' age or physical condition. Clearly, it is not more expensive than the cost of an employee who is idle and waiting for someone to bring a book to a circulation desk for check out. It is less expensive than the cost of calling or mailing a message to inform someone that resources are sitting idle and waiting to be picked up.

ECONOMIC ADVANTAGES OF BOOKS BY MAIL

Suppose that you just arrived from another planet and observed this country and its public libraries. You would wonder why it was necessary for an individual to leave the house, get in an expensive car, burn gas, create exhaust fumes, contribute to the traffic mess, get frustrated with parking, enter the building, check out a book, and then repeat the process over again when the book was due for return. You would have to conclude that the book must be something very special. The social and economic cost of the process is remarkable. But it has been done this way for decades, and that is the only durable and apparent reason for it to continue.

Big corporations, publishers, advertisers and even smaller businesses are using the mail to deliver their message more than at any time in history. The United Parcel Service, couriers, Brinks, and Federal Express are among the many services which are thriving as they deliver documents and packages. More are just getting started. Magazines, newspapers, and bulk mailers are into alternative, less expensive delivery methods which are beyond those mentioned. The cost of delivering services has gone up over the years and that is doubtless

a big reason why other services have arrived on the scene and will continue to do so. Many people are able to acquire information and text via electronic means, and the number will increase in the future. Libraries must recognize that users need delivery, for society understands the necessity. We have shopping by television and mail. Meals are delivered to the home. Drive-up services are liberally available. There are more and more cars, and fewer and fewer sidewalks.

THE EFFICIENCY OF BOOKS BY MAIL

Industry has demonstrated long before we were born that repetitive processes can be designed to be very efficient, particularly in relation to processes which are random or inconsistent. Efficiency applied to checking out books in a back room is a vastly different thing than, for example, somehow inducing the public at the circulation desk to maintain a constant line to keep the circulation clerk busy and to avoid things which impede efficiency. Libraries are there to provide one thing for the users, a book or other item. Without rationalization, there are more ways than one to check out a book. Most libraries already involve the Postal Service in some form of library service. Haven't most users who reserve a book received a card in the mail advising them that there is a book waiting for them at the library?

The USPS is obliged to carry the mail. They try to accomplish their duties efficiently. Users with significant mail will get every consideration from the Postal Service. Pickup, delivery, boxes, bins, bags—whatever it takes to do the job, and wherever the interests converge. The question is not should we do it, but rather how can we do it efficiently. Twenty years ago mail carriers physically carried more mail on their backs. Today, the USPS uses more vehicles to help the carriers in their deliveries. This and other changes in postal service and alternative delivery methods should convince more libraries to evaluate and adopt direct delivery.

COSTS

Postage currently averages more than a dollar per hardback book. That expense and other costs associated with delivery may have been prohibitive in the early days of mailing, but times have changed. The basic materials required for delivery, such as bags and labels, are economical when they are purchased in quantity. Space is not a critical issue as long as there is a little space that could be appropriated or shared. In larger operations, the process is eased considerably if the space is near a loading dock. If the library mails books in greater quantity, consideration should be given to bagging by zip code. The Postal Service can provide the equipment for simplified handling for quantity mailers using this procedure. This may consist of rolling racks which hold bags open for continuous sorting and wire cages for bulk handling of mail bags. The USPS offers an array of special services to help their customers. For example, one new Postal Service innovation can guarantee that your books will be delivered overnight.

Comparing books by mail with traditional library procedures, at least one step would be eliminated. The necessity to notify the user just disappears. The cost of staff, telephone, post card, fee, computer and anything else that goes into the traditional notification procedure is eliminated. Once the users have told the library what they want, and the library has confirmed the availability of the material, it can be checked out to them, put into the mail, and never handled separately again. The process is no longer one of handling exceptions, which is what we do now. We can place the special handling of reserves into the routines of the day. There are undeniable efficiencies in the concept.

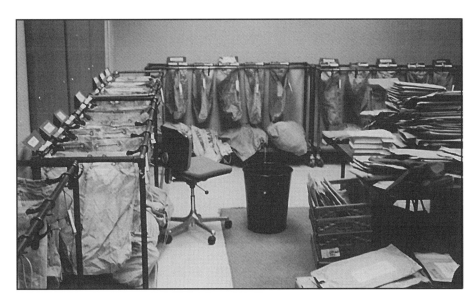

Illustration 13.1: Racks and mail bags can be used to improve the efficiency of large mail operations.

LOSSES

Would more books be lost through books by mail? It has been my experience that the losses are similar to losses for books which are checked out at the circulation desk. It could be argued that the control is actually better because delivery confirms the accuracy of the borrower's mailing address. A bad address results in returned mail. Has the Postal Service ever lost a book? Probably so, but we know for certain that considerable loss occurs right over the circulation desk. I believe the Postal Service will lose far fewer books than we experience using traditional circulation procedures.

How much does it cost? That depends a great deal on the ingenuity of the managers. Will the Postal Service handle our books by mail program? They certainly can and if they won't, others will. Do we have the space? This does not require much space, certainly for a test. Will the public accept it? The recipients love it. Does the public want it? Yes, if the overall cost of library service does not go up. Does it cost too much? In the mix of services, no. Will the press report it favorably? Yes, if they are

included in the process. Does the staff accept it? Once it is demonstrated that there is no risk to the staff, it is well accepted.

PROGRAM REQUIREMENTS

What does a books by mail program require? A mail service can be tested quite easily and without any major budget reallocation. Some padded jiffy bags, mailing labels, postage scales and stamps are all that is required. Regardless of how you handle reserves and notification of the user, the library must have the user's requested book and the correct name and address. The major difference is that rather than notifying users that their book is now available and waiting, it is mailed directly to them. No further handling is required. There is no more waiting for notification, remembering to visit the library, driving to the library, waiting for service, engaging a public employee (maybe more than one), checking out the book, and then repeating the transportation process.

There are many techniques and labor-saving ideas which could be employed to expe-

Illustration 13.2: Postage meters, adhesive labels and padded bags can be used to expedite mailing operations.

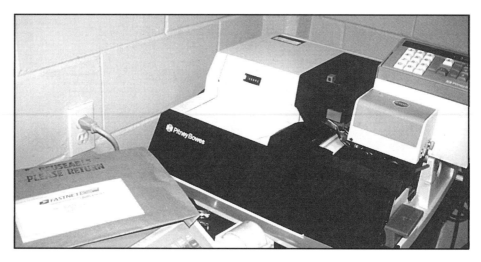

CUSTOMER SERVICE & INNOVATION IN LIBRARIES

dite and simplify the mailing process. However, every library has different staffing requirements and facilities. Every library has ample motivation and competence to introduce labor-saving techniques and efficiency into the process. There are likely to be many major mailers in most cities and communities, and they may be willing to offer advice or at least a tour of their facilities to demonstrate how they are able to process large mailings. Pre-printed labels, postage machines, terminal access to the library's circulation and public catalog systems, bulk purchasing of supplies, convenient storage of supplies, a thorough knowledge of postal regulations, liaison with local USPS personnel; these and others are the ingredients of large scale mailing. The USPS is willing and eager to consult with you when the results mean more business for them.

INTRODUCING THE PROGRAM

The public is reasonable and it will be more than willing to accept thoughtful change, especially if they are the beneficiaries. Just as surely, there may be individuals who will be indignant and shrill in their condemnation of any dramatic change in traditional library service. By comparison, name the politician, local or otherwise, who was elected unanimously. It has never happened, just as our service and changes to it have never been received unanimously. Keep in mind that the positives in your life tend to be taken for granted and the negatives generate frustration and anger. It was ever so and we aren't likely to easily change it.

The library staff will be the group that will experience the most traumatic change in introducing books by mail. They will be most affected because some of them will find that their work assignments will be altered. There are emotional feelings, conscious or unconscious, that go to the heart of one's usefulness and role in any institution. Any change of this nature may lead to a loss of self-esteem, especially if a new assignment is significantly different, such as a transfer from public service to mail processing. All staff will be affected in some way. Preparation, training and information are important all the time. In times of significant change, greater staff awareness and involvement are vital. Even then, everyone may not accept the change. Under those circumstances, provide means for the staff most directly involved to have access to the public reactions. Most employees will intellectually accept change if there is clear evidence that the users are receptive. If fan mail from the public is something you like to receive, then a books by mail program is probably going to generate more than most services.

14 AUTODELIVERY

Libraries need to consider *automatically* mailing books to their users, particularly to those users with special needs. Often, it is the most practical outreach method. It is fundamentally reasonable and not difficult to accomplish. Automatic mailing of books came to the Orange County Library System in Florida as the result of an innocent phone call from a librarian to a manager. A conversation something like this ensued.

Librarian to manager: "Mr. T is upset and says he is going to call you about his complaint. It seems that he does not like the process of calling and talking to librarians about what he wants to read. He is not that fussy and thinks it is a waste of time to have a lot of conversation about it, especially with tax-paid employees."

Manager to librarian: "What can we do about it?"

Librarian: "I merely told him the policy. I thought you would like to have forewarning if he should directly call you, for he was upset."

Manager: "Thanks. You are right, it is helpful to know."

From such a trivial and routine exchange, a significant program of service delivery was born. The manager thought about the patron's complaint and asked himself: Why don't we send Mr. T. his books on a regular basis using our knowledge of what he seems to prefer to read? Or, even better, why don't we share with him titles of books that we know we have in immediate supply?

We've never done anything quite like that before and neither, apparently, has any other library. No elected official, and few others, would permit the library to send material in the mail when individuals can go to the library and get it themselves. How could we justify sending books when some selections may turn out to be books the user has already read? The library cannot afford to be a personal shopper for anyone who wants the service. We don't have enough staff to do such a thing.

THE CHALLENGE OF CHANGE

We're often faced with challenges like this whenever a new idea arises, and we often wonder whether it can be done. Normally, we give up the idea, for there is no use in having such dreams when the deck is so stacked against you. Nobody would let you get past all of the negative rationale which would come your way. The library paradigm does not include such off-the-wall kind of service.

But wait, why are we here? Isn't Mr. T a taxpayer? Is he not the reason for our professional existence? Let's slow down a bit and review the process again. What does he want? He wants his tax-paid employees to get him some of the books we purchased with his tax funds. That is neither pejorative nor outlandish. That is what we think we are doing. Why does it sound like he is making unreasonable demands of us? I suspect that it is several things. It bothers us when someone asks for something which we cannot produce. It is dangerously like pointing out our limitations when we feel we already go 100 percent of the way. We are accustomed to serving all who come to us.

That's another thing, he doesn't want to come to us. Everybody always comes to us. We don't come to you, you come to us. Select? Why should we select everything an individual wants to read? There are so many choices and we don't know what someone's read. It would be expensive and wasteful. It's just not the way library service is given.

Is it really Mr. T's desire that is unsettling? Maybe it is our reaction to it. We may well not be able to accommodate Mr. T, but on the other hand, we could apply some creative thinking to the situation. After all,

aren't we already applying significant time to the process of helping people find books that they haven't read based on their general reading preferences? We have been suggesting and getting titles all of our working lives, and the library has been doing it for a hundred years. Does that collective experience include automatically selecting and mailing books to users? Unfortunately, we've done very little of it, and therein lies much of the difficulty with innovation. Are we willing to draw attention to ourselves and risk the possibility of being wrong? Will we lose face, respect or worse?

AUTOMATIC MAILING SERVICE

Mailing books was discussed in the previous chapter. Adopting the procedure may be a big hurdle in some libraries, but mailing them automatically presents some hurdles of its own. We do not generally buy enough copies of a title in order to have the resources to launch such a program. That, too, was the subject of a previous chapter. Even with relatively few copies of sufficient titles a library can experiment.

Collect the copies of titles for which the highest demand has passed. Make a list of these books and select a test group of users. Ask the users to examine the list and indicate which titles they would like to read. We all have written or made mental lists of books we would like to read someday but never seem to have the time. The primary reason we never read them is because we have never had them in our hands. We do not have the time to go to the library as many of us once did. A typical reader may well find five or thirty titles they haven't read out of 50 or 100 or so popular books from the last couple of years.

we're talking about books which individuals want to read, not necessarily those that we think would be good for them to read.

AUTOMATING RECORDS

The process for keeping track of readers and selections is routine for librarians and it has good potential as a computer application. Those librarians who use computer programs in the delivery of talking books for the blind and physically handicapped are acquainted with the labor-saving possibilities. Automating delivery is similar. The user list can be stored and manipulated. Mailing labels are handled quite easily with computers and printers. The tracking of choices and recording of those books already received by a user is somewhat more complex but still quite possible.

DELIVERY COSTS

What about the cost for postage? Some may believe this will be too expensive. Libraries are paying a fair amount already, even assuming they use book rate. Equal access to the resources shouldn't apply to only those who are able to come to the library building. The United States Postal Service (USPS) is being beset with competitors today and one result is the USPS is becoming more competitive and receptive to change. There may be other companies that offer a better alternative for delivering books. If we indeed are efficient managers, we'll stay abreast of the options.

This method of selecting and delivering books is more than a different slant on traditional service. This is a conceptually different delivery system that does not require individuals to come to the library building to get library service. Further, they do not

Illustration 14.1: A collection of several copies of a number of titles which are no longer in great demand can be the basis of a test of autodelivery.

Frankly, the logistics are simple. Librarians have made card files for years and now we can do it on computers. Just like talking books for the blind, we can maintain the files to keep track of the books a reader has received and the books still on a want list. All that remains is to determine how often the reader would like to receive a book–weekly, bi-weekly, monthly, or whatever is reasonable that can be delivered. Note that need to even think about it regularly. The library can well use taxpayers' money to change the basic methods of fulfilling its mission through the development and testing of innovative services such as automatic mail. Taxpayers pay for the building. They pay for the salaries. They pay for the books, and wouldn't they be tickled when book selections show up with virtually zero inconvenience or effort on their part. Taking a broad perspective, this service may well be a more effective expenditure than many services we now provide.

We can provide our users with books and eliminate the costly interface and exchange with a librarian each time it happens. Try it and witness the benefits for the readers and the savings for the library.

15 KIDSMAIL

Children are our future, and we know that reading spurs their development. The public library should be inspiring children and finding more creative ways to put books into their hands. This chapter is about one innovative program that I call Kidsmail.

There is probably general agreement in our society that kids are the most valuable asset that we have. Many groups vie for the title of most concerned or most knowledgeable on the subject of children. Who can argue with their motivation? We want children to be great and confident and capable. We want them to achieve some of the goals that we weren't able to attain. We want them to be independent, and we want them to stay out of trouble. We want them to have good families. We just want everything for them. The public library represents much that is good for children. Literature, ideas, thought, study, language, learning and more are all there.

THE LIBRARY'S ROLE

We urge parents to take their children to the library and good things will happen. The youngsters are exposed to the world through books, story times, movies, tapes, fingerplays, and much more. They are introduced to the community, librarians, and other public employees. All of that is good. Arguably, the kids who are taken to the library are getting a better exposure to life. Unfortunately, it does not have much impact on the lives of *some* kids. For example, it doesn't help the kids who don't read. It doesn't help the kids who don't visit the library regularly.

The motivation of librarians to help children is unquestioned. What might be questioned is how the motivation is translated into action. Every day, we hear that children from disadvantaged homes just do not have literature around the house, and therefore the possibilities and influences at home are not conducive to reading. It has been said just as many times that every child needs a parent or role model in the home who reads, in order to set a good example for the child. Educators and sociologists have long debated the factors and circumstances that motivate a child to read. Whatever research reveals about reading, librarians are convinced that reading can open the imagination and spur the pursuit of more reading. In the process, almost everything that happens is positive, and that is why we foster reading for children.

For all but the recent generation, visiting the library was an almost routine exercise. There was limited concern about children being out of sight of a parent. Children could and did walk to their library. Society was not as complex as it is today. Because of the increasing number of single parent families, the prevalence of day care, and households where both parents work, the children of this generation are often dependent upon individuals outside the family for a greater share of their guidance and development. Librarians are among those outsiders.

Public libraries have invested in services and collections for children. We buy more books and we have more storytimes. We network with other agencies. We will do anything for those children–as long as what we do doesn't differ too much from what we have done all along. Like many other professions that serve children, we do not find it easy to change. Change is so difficult that we frequently do a great deal of adjusting so that we really don't have to change. We tinker and dabble. We change the appearance of our services, but not the substance. If we checked our youth programs carefully and compared them to what we offered ten years ago, we would find that

virtually all of the changes have been superficial.

BARRIERS TO THE LIBRARY

If you were a child who was just being awakened to the world of reading but had nothing to read, what would you do? Of course, we hope that you knew about the library, and would consider a visit. Some children may be fortunate enough to be within walking distance of a library, and live in a community where it would be safe enough to go there by themselves. Some children may even have parents and relatives able to buy books for them. Unfortunately, I believe these children are in a minority in our society. Most children are dependent upon a caregiver to take them to the library. Even a wealthy family would be unable to buy all the educational resources a child needs, or have the time to acquire them. Access to a library, therefore, is important to every child's development.

What happens when the parent or caregiver lacks the time, transportation, or motivation to take a child to the library? For many children there may be no one nearby who places a priority upon the need to read. And, the priority isn't enough. The caregiver has to possess a whole list of capabilities that would significantly raise the prospects of getting books into hands of the child. The answer is that there is a need for alternative services that can extend the library into the home. One such option is to mail books to children.

MAIL SERVICE

It is relatively easy to figure out which children's titles are available in paperback editions. Every library is capable of

Illustration 14.1 Multiple copies of popular children's resources are one of the basic requirements.

determining the contents of a preferred list of books comprised of twenty-four titles for children ages four to eleven. Every library has a means for determining, with some effectiveness, children who might profit more than others by receiving librarian-selected books in the home. Is there a negative side to putting books directly into the hands of children? None that I know. The absolute worst thing that could happen is that the books never reappear in the library. If that happens we can take considerable solace in the fact that there is a book in a house at the disposal of a child who probably would have few or none otherwise. This program could be the win-win situation that every public agency hopes for.

Would the library ever know what the effect would be? Probably not. Does the library know the effect of not checking books out to people? No, not really. Is there any reason to believe that a child without books would not be as interested in a book as a child with plenty of books? We don't know,

frankly. Does the mission of the library foster or preclude mailing books to children? It does not. Would the community find it to be good or bad? It would be a pretty heartless person who would find it less desirable than much of what we do. Many libraries already sponsor some form of this program by giving free books to selected groups or classifications of children. By any measure, it would be in the interest of the community, the government, the library and especially the children to mail books to them at their home.

IMPLEMENTING THE SERVICE

There are practical considerations that make such a program attractive. There are many paperback editions of popular children's books to accommodate the scope of such a program if the library mails, for example, two books per month to a child. The cost of paperbacks is attractive by comparison with the cost of hardcover or library-bound editions. The cost of mailing paperbacks is significantly less than postage for hardcovers just by virtue of weight. Because of their attractive covers, paperbacks lose little of the aesthetic qualities of their hardcover counterparts. Paperbacks are easier to handle and fit better into a backpack. The youngsters don't care which version they read. When they are ready to read, they will read anything.

I would recommend that the age of each child participating in the service be obtained so that the books can be selected to match the child's appropriate reading level. Once set up, a monthly rotation can be handled easily. Some librarians have experience in selecting and automatic mailing of talking books for persons with reading disabilities, such as the blind and physically disabled, and this can serve as a good example. The talking books program has employed a manual system for this, but automated programs are now available, and they could be easily adapted for use with Kidsmail. Another option would be to write your own software, or to hire a consultant to write and implement a computerized program to maintain the necessary records.

Organizing the mailing procedures for Kidsmail does not require a genius. Some jiffy bags, a little printing, some postage, a minor investment in paperback books, some staff time reassigned from an infrequently used program, and you are in business.

EVALUATING THE SERVICE

Don't expect the children to write you letters for the smile file. This program will operate best on faith that you are just doing the right thing. The worst thing that can happen to the library is that there would be a few books that would not be returned. I don't believe this would be a significant problem. Libraries lose thousands of books to adults who are irresponsible. It helps to keep it all in perspective. In a Head Start group in Orange County, Florida, where this program is available, the coordinator reported one unanticipated bonus. Some non-reading parents became readers, and others were able to improve their skills in order to read the books to their young children.

In these times when so many are concerned about the educational development and welfare of our children, the importance of reading, and strengthening the family, why haven't more libraries initiated programs such as Kidsmail? I believe that many communities would approve this service by a landslide if they had a chance to do so. However, it hasn't received the blessing of conformity. If others aren't doing it, the media or the government, or some other group, doesn't approve. Will it be tried? Maybe, if your library does it.

16 OUTLETS

The traditional branch library is not getting the job done. While we operate branch libraries today better than we ever did in the past, these service units are not effectively reaching potential users. We must change the concept and the reality of community extension and access to library service.

The various ideas and possibilities presented on the following pages would create an interesting and useful library which should attract more people. A library "outlet" is an alternative to a branch library which emphasizes efficiency and public convenience. This outlet would be on a main thoroughfare for automobile access, have a generous amount of free parking, utilize a drive-up window, have continuous storytelling, offer meeting rooms, contain a browsing collection of current material, and function during hours almost completely at the convenience of the users.

ACCESS AND TRAFFIC

Try not to use traditional words to describe the outlet. Set it apart as something entirely different from a branch library. There are libraries with some of these features, but few offer all of them.

If there is a corner in your community with significant traffic which supports shopping and services, that is the most likely site for an outlet. Storytelling sessions attract large audiences, and to accommodate them we need access and easy, ample parking. We need parking for school buses. If bus drivers can get in and out and have simple, easy parking, they would be pleased to deliver children. Schools and teachers would be more likely to schedule class visits because of the accessibility, frequency, and predictability of the programs. For similar reasons it would be easier for parents to bring their children. Location is important because ease of access is generally as critical as distance. The site also requires good traffic safety conditions for both pedestrians and drivers.

Ample free parking is another requirement, but it still isn't the key to the success of an outlet. The parking must be laid out so that internal traffic is clear and easy with a minimum of congestion. There will be people coming and going all the time. The front door and the drive-up window must have careful consideration. They do not need to be next to each other, although proximity could affect staff efficiency. The potential line of cars waiting for the window must not create a problem in the parking lot or users will find that it isn't worth the hassle.

The outlet needs a large sidewalk with overhead weather protection. These sidewalks are for passenger waiting and pickup. Buses will merit major consideration. There should be a specified drop-off space for buses. Bus parking should be within fifty yards and in sight of the front door. There should be consideration for vans and small buses in the form of adjacent parking with ample loading and unloading space. Lighting should be sufficient to turn the area into daylight.

DRIVE-UP WINDOW

The location of the drive-up window must be easily apparent to drivers, and the driver's car window should be level with the drive-up window. A bank window may serve as a good model of the drive-up window concept, recognizing that there is more bulk to books than in money. Excellent communication capability is needed between the driver and the employee behind the glass, even if it is only a natural, but baffled, opening. Don't overlook the fast food solutions which have openings as opposed to drawers. Inside the drive-up window everything should be designed for function, function, function. There must be

greater space because more types of lending will occur than we have previously considered. The exterior of the drive-up window must be defensively protected against careless drivers and tall trucks. The extended book tray/box should be protected by a pylon or curb so it cannot be hit by a car. The drive-up window should have an overhang which keeps off the sun and the rain, but it must be high enough so that a truck or van cannot hit it.

LOBBY

The lobby of the outlet may be more reminiscent of a theater lobby than anything you may have previously seen in a library. Beyond the entrance and weather lock is a lobby with some seating. Dominating the interior is a supervisory island. From the island, library employees will have visual control over the entire library including lobby, corridors and browsing collection. On one side of the lobby there should be an entry to the browsing and lending library. Glass would make an appropriate wall between the lobby and the browsing library so that staff could see most of the space at all times. The island should serve as a circulation desk, book return station, and it may even double as a bookstore. Why not let the users borrow or buy a book that was featured during a story session. Have you noticed that many newer book stores are beginning to look more like libraries? There should be space in the outlet for coffee and soda vending, and this might appear in the lobby.

The lobby and corridor areas need to be large enough to provide queuing and staging areas for groups of children. The use of stanchions and velour-covered rope is desirable for upcoming storytelling. Some children can be waiting in specific spaces for upcoming programs while others could be awaiting school buses or the parent who brought them. No one would be surprised at a sound system. If a child is ready and the parent is nowhere in sight, a speaker announcement would reach the browsing library, restrooms and the front entry area, notifying everyone that a certain program has ended and participants can be collected.

CHILDREN'S STORYTELLING

Storytelling is one of the driving forces of the outlet. Libraries will never have a more important role than introducing children to good literature. Our job is to make it pleasant and inspiring. The storytellers should be chosen specifically for their skills and ability to develop rapport with their audience. If they are staff, their primary responsibility should be storytelling and all other assignments minimized so that they can prepare and refine their presentations. One of the goals should be to reach as many children as possible. Storytelling should be scheduled during time periods that are most convenient for users, and programs might be offered every twenty or twenty-five minutes. Other times or schedules may be specially arranged in advance but within guidelines that enhance efficiency.

All programs and meetings should be scheduled ahead of time with predictable patterns for weeks or months in advance. The more focused the library's mission, the easier it will be to carry it out effectively and efficiently. It would be nice to be all things to all people whenever they wished, but

responsibility and accountability dictate that we be circumspect in this regard.

The rooms will need to be designed with care. The ability to have movement in, through and out in an efficient manner is paramount. Groups should be collected, held and then ushered into the rooms. This can avoid confusion and conflicts of space while the children are prepared for the session. The storytelling rooms must have acoustical treatment so there is a minimum of conflicting noise from elsewhere in the outlet. The rooms may have two separate doors, one for entry and one for exiting. The doors must be wide enough so that tables and chairs can be moved freely and to avoid delay in filling or emptying the room. When the rooms are not being used for storytelling they will be available as public meeting rooms. Consideration should be given to storage of tables and chairs in addition to the necessary program and cleaning equipment.

COLLECTION

The browsing collection is one of the library's most important features to its long-time users. It is a mainstay, and nothing will ever replace browsing for a devoted reader. To maintain good circulation, the collection must be current and popular. That will also mean that the collection may be relatively small, 20,000 to 30,000 volumes. Shelf maintenance should be conducted entirely for the user. All materials must be easy to see and reach. Three-quarter height (60") shelves are logical as long as the bottom shelves are not utilized. Some of these shelves will contain the stories and fables featured during the storytelling sessions as well as classic children's books. Adult materials will be popular fiction and nonfiction.

Reference? Here is a tough paradigm shift. There will be no significant reference collection housed in the outlet. The rationale is not too different from some popular libraries. The potential use does not warrant the expense of the staff and resources. In order to be truly useful as a reference collection there needs to be substantial resources as well as an area for extended use. If reference is meaningful, there must be competent, and therefore expensive, librarians to implement the process. The conventional library assumptions must be tested.

However, reference service can be given over the telephone or through an online computer. If a patron is going to call a branch, for example, it is just as easy to call the main library which has a larger concentration of skilled librarians and a superior collection. A person can also go to a branch which has conventional reference capability. That is still available to users. Given those alternatives, the reference service in the outlet can be minimized. Reference requests will be accommodated by providing the users with telephones or computer terminals that provide direct access to the system's main reference department. Branch reference collections have often been criticized because they are too modest to do the job.

Branch library service is popular in many communities, but the time has come to reassess the effectiveness of traditional branch library services and collections. Changes in society such as increased mobility, extended business hours, and improved telecommunications merit a reconsideration of existing branch operations.

INDEX